SWEET CONFLUENCE

SWEET CONFLUENCE

New and Selected Poems

Susan Ludvigson

Louisiana State University Press · Baton Rouge MM

This collection is dedicated to
the memory of my parents.

Manufactured in the United States of America
First printing
09 08 07 06 05 04 03 02 01 00
5 4 3 2 1

Designer: Laura Roubique Gleson
Typeface: Minion
Typesetter: Coghill Composition Co.
Printer and binder: Thomson-Shore, Inc.

Library of Congress Cataloging-in-Publication Data

Ludvigson, Susan.
   Sweet confluence : new and selected poems / Susan Ludvigson.
      p. cm.
   ISBN 0-8071-2619-5 (cloth : alk. paper)—ISBN 0-8071-2620-9 (pbk. : alk. paper)
      I. Title.
   PS3562.U27   S84   2000
   811'.54—dc21
                                                            00-032743

Poems herein have been selected from *Trinity* (Louisiana State University Press, 1996),
Everything Winged Must Be Dreaming (Louisiana State University Press, 1993), *To Find the Gold*
(Louisiana State University Press, 1990), *The Beautiful Noon of No Shadow* (Louisiana State
University Press, 1986), *The Swimmer* (Louisiana State University Press, 1984), and *Northern
Lights* (Louisiana State University Press, 1981). The author wishes to thank the editors of the
following publications, in which some of the new poems, or versions of them, first appeared:
Georgia Review, Gettysburg Review, Midwest Quarterly, Ohio Review, Poetry, Shenandoah.
   "Varieties of Angels" first appeared in *The Ninety-Six Sampler of South Carolina Poetry,* ed.
Gilbert Allen (Greenville, SC: Ninety-Six Press).

My thanks to Dannye Powell, Julie Suk, Lucinda Grey, Mary Hunter Daly, Judy Goldman, and
the late Harriet Doar for their helpful criticism of poems. And my thanks to Nicola Mason, for
her keen eye and judicious editing of the manuscript.

The paper in this book meets the guidelines for permanence and durability of the Committee on
Production Guidelines for Book Longevity of the Council on Library Resources. ⊗

Perhaps you will say: Are you sure this legend is true? Does it matter what the reality outside me may be if it has helped me to live, to feel sure that I am and what I am?

—Charles Baudelaire, "Les Fenêtres," *Petits Poèmes en Prose*

CONTENTS

BECAUSE I AM LUCKY

For Kathryn Kirkpatrick

because I grew up
in a small midwestern town
where, when the snow melted
and the loam of thawed fields
was turned over, the seeds
cast into it were not certainties
so much as hopes

because I was a first child, bossy,
red-haired, allowed to settle
family questions of right,
to make judgments on movies
and grammar, to say when the ice
on the lake was too thin for skating

because I knew everything
until childhood sank
into the dark pond of adolescence,
and when I was pulled out
gasping and spitting I was married
and had a son

because the magician who saved me
wore a mask,
stood far enough away
that I couldn't say He or She

because the spells
rephrased themselves
until I believed I had
invented them

because, alone in a forest at dusk,
I picked my way over rocks
in winter streams
and never broke an ankle

because tongues I had no gift for
began whispering riddles

I could not decipher,
but I heard the music arriving
as if from underwater

because there were days
I would have walked
into the wide St. Croix
where it merges
with the Mississippi
but the evergreens
on the other side
were speaking a language
I thought I recognized

because I have passed the middle
of my life and finally see how
in the currents of words
and water I learned to swim

because in dreams there are floods
still, and suddenly opened dams
that sweep me away from the banks,
and fear that wakes me as voices
say what I understand only later
when they dive through the places
I can seldom reach

because I know that this, too,
is luck, no matter what else, every time,
and that the river keeps rising.

New Poems

THE LILIES OF LANDSFORD CANAL

Twenty years I've lived
    so near a miracle
        it's possible to bicycle there.

(Not me, so out of shape a walk up a long hill leaves me
breathless, but my fit neighbor says so.)

In canoes we navigate the stony shoals,
    shores and islands green
        as a long-remembered dream.

But where are the promised lilies?

I thought they'd be like Monet's,
    floating flat at the edge of a river
        under the shadow of willows bending
            to riffle the water.

The others think we must be too late, must have missed
    the season.

A few clumps of tall grasses
    have stalks with possible buds, or maybe
        they're the stubble of flowers now blown

        by the wind toward shore,

    but in any case, there's nothing like blooms
anywhere.

Then we round a bend and there they are—choirs

    swaying in a rhythm to the moving water.

        They are singing hosannas, a music

so ecstatic and silent it has to be white.

Whole islands are massed with them, long stems and dark
        embracing leaves like French genêts,
but the delicate spiked white blossoms are enormous
    and complex

as stars through a telescope. They shine against
      the skittering silver water,
               against the trembling wall of green behind,
                    against the stones rising up

in the shallows, seeming, by contrast, fragile.

But no.

                              They grow wild
                  in just a few places in the world.

A thousand years old, against the odds,
               they repeat themselves year after year

                        like swallows or salmon returning home.

I rarely enter anything like their world.

Even when we're past

      that shimmering, the Catawba wider
               and smoother than before, the air is fragrant

as a childhood summer.

Surely there is no more innocence here than anywhere.
Downstream, I'm told, the river is polluted by chemicals.

Yet I feel as if I'm entering something pure,
         some place not wholly exterior. I knew it once,
                  I think, but so long ago it has ceased to be.

Islands of lilies live so close
            I could have watched them open
                    every year.

I could have kept them where closed eyes
         would bring them back, white plumes
                  soothing the air.

For twenty summers

I could have picnicked on these and other banks

         where canoes glide by, some of their passengers, like me,
               late discovering their lives.

GRATITUDE

The body is a boat gliding
down the river whose fragrance
spins us to the shady places
under apple trees
and into bedrooms. When
it ties up at shore,
the soul drifts and returns.

More and more I see
how everything goes together.
There is such grace in this reconciliation—
even the stomach, that restless
loner, begins to understand.

Surely the body is mind's
gift to the soul. How else
would the dance of ecstasy begin,
except in the muscles, in how
the eyes light on beauty
and expand it, blue
when it needs blue.

Think how love penetrates
like music, rhythm
overpowering stasis
as the nerves, the pulse,
propel us toward moonlight,
and how the body celebrates
wholeness, its first desire.

WHERE SNOW FALLS

For Sun and Michael

Buried in your letter from Sweden:
"I get slowly more deaf and now can hardly
hear the snow falling."

Your country is a memory I've longed
to enter, a tunnel
whose exit opens and opens
to a painless birth

where snow falls with such a tenderness
it's home.

When it mounds on roofs I imagine
the piano's soft pedal,
the house changing mood.

Wisconsin was foreplay,
wind teasing it out of trees,
drifts hiding
whatever chooses muteness,
that erotic slate
of possibilities.

We knew it by sighs into windows,
its body shifting in sleep.

Where you are, it has
a voice deeper than a man's.

I have lain down in it
and tempted what masquerades
as warmth,

heard rumors
so persuasive, I think
my cheeks were meant to burn.

VARIETIES OF ANGELS

The room is so full of light,
it's as if angels had collected
on the lawn, their tremulous wings
reflecting all the sun there is—
hardly enough for an ordinary day
in March, but on this one
of rare southern snow,
it reflects, even through clouds,
another world's brightness.
It woke me from the dream
of near-betrayal. A beautiful man
lay at my side, an angel.
But when he put his hands on my breasts,
I said no. Only his words
could be allowed to drift
over my body, warming it
the way snow warms the earth
in cold country, where as a child
I made angels enough to accompany me
to another life. I had almost forgotten
how snow silences much that intrudes
on the streets of any neighborhood.
And yet this is not peace,
but the body's yearning to lie
in that bliss of white, arms and legs
fanning slowly, until the skin begins
to redden and tingle, signs that tell us
we're dying, and that we're still alive.

SOMEDAY THE WICKER CHAIRS

before the café in Quillan's square
will disappear. Glasses of citron
pressé on the marble tables
will evaporate with the words
we read there. We'll forget
the fish market, the man
who promised salmon from the mountains
cold as a swimmer's kiss. And how low
the river was, where rocks lifted
like heads from the shallow water,
multiple late-summer births. We'll lose
the puffed brioche and the quail,
fresh-killed, in the old glass case,
the young man in the bank
combing his thin hair, practicing
English, and how the shut hotel
beckoned year after year, its porches
cool, its refusals mysterious
and dark as memory.

AFTER GATSBY

Whatever attributes objects might possess are
contextual.
      —John L. Custi, *Paradigms Lost*

In the museum of the heart,
the most inauspicious things are placed
on pedestals. If I said
this bench, this stone table,
invite a world to reassemble itself,
you might not know the movie
from my childhood, the miracle
of a garden, walled, with dreaming
shadows, and cannot know
how the branches of a pecan
arch over us, a canopy
of sieved and moving light.

A vanity in a secondhand shop,
its surface stained with cold cream
and perfume, a heavy white porcelain mug,
the print of an English cottage
framed in gold, are more
than the furniture of nostalgia.
They occupy a continuous world
where value is as various
as the people who walk in
jingling the bell on the door,
minds leaning toward invention.

WHAT YOU MEANT

And when my vision turned to the right
looking out over the sea
to a stand of trees, I thought
that was what you meant, where
you were pointing, but no, the miracle
was to the left, where the moon lifted
out of its stillness a ring of water
circling and circling into the sky,
that silver looping itself under shattering
light performing its strange
gravitational trick, a once-
in-a-lifetime enactment
of something we wanted to think of
as carnival, like a small Ferris wheel
risen out of the water, a white celebration
against the black drop of the night
where it shone and spun even after we turned
and went back to our lives

SO MANY WAYS TO TELL
OURSELVES THE TRUTHS

that beg for silence, like walking
in a hayfield after the cutting, or swimming
farther out than your strength makes safe.
Sometimes you wake with a longing
for something that escaped
with childhood: the swiftness
of August storm, a whistling man
unsaddling a roan, the leather
wet. His is the voice
of dream when the film goes on.
Last night it stopped midscene—
your legs lifted, you removing
stockings. Often truth trails
out of sight, like a girl's long hair
waving behind her, only ripples of air
coming back, never the scent
of the past in a shape you could follow.
You go more slowly than you did
through the leaves, weep at the sudden
sight of men on horseback. One tips
his hat. Never again your father.

THIS MOVE INTO THE ABSTRACT

Why go into that dark-walled room
where mind, holding
a crystal scepter,
insists on its authority—
what portion of the self
could it satisfy? Surely not
the brain, that lover
of sensation, organ
whose chords are made to swell
by the sweet confluence
of salt and sun, of ache
and thrust.

Think of goosebumps on the skin
when the heart's weather changes,
when a clash of systems
funnels the past
to new configurations—trees
upside down, so that mazes
of roots become exotic bouquets
and roofs fly, rearranging dreams.
We want to see those chairs
and beds upended, in different
rooms, want that wind singing
in our ears, want flesh
lifted into air by the magnetic
force of other flesh.

We know how the parts of the body
deceive themselves,
we need not rehearse
what masquerades as love.
Let us not humor, either,
the notion of ideas floating in their own
no-trespassing pool:
let's turn the heat off,
wait for the sun to go down.

LISTENING

Shadow, shadow, the heart says,
racing itself, racing the rain.

You are the side I seldom
turn to, though we glide down
the same halls every day
and you confide in me
as if light held an answer.

If there are answers,
I am learning them slowly,
learning to trust
what cannot say its name.

The heart by some other name
would be a simpler mechanism,
its echoes reverberating
less wildly.

Call it a blood pump
and it loses its voice,
that husky whisper you hear
in your sleep. No,
I have no answers, only
the slower pulse
by which
I live now, at peace,
the only sign of the past
a risky murmur.

THE BRAIN ENJOYS ITS
SECRET LIFE

Humming through a morning,
hoeing the radishes, you let drift
your mother's admonitions.
You turn them over like soil
and then forget, going on
to the baking. All the while
scenes are being played
behind a curtain.
Now and then you hear
a whispered cue, but the play
is background noise,
like a radio station interfering
with the one you tuned in
hours before. With the denouement,
you start whistling,
your father's warble
surprising you from your own
mouth that never before
knew birdsong.

A DAY LIKE ANY OTHER

Except that the fields are undulations
of red and lavender. It must be
a kind of heather, I say aloud,
driving past, the word
caressing the wind coming up,
coming in the window. I imagine
heaths when the sun goes behind clouds
and April gives itself over to the past
while inventing a future
fraught with consequence.
Farther south, a deep green landscape
waits for the man whose vision
is enlarged, the horizon disappearing
as if he'd dreamed himself
toward paradise. The woman's heaven
is somewhere else, in Paris,
where chestnut trees are barely
coming into bud, where breezes
carry gusts of syllables
to a courtyard where she drinks
hot chocolate, the fire-breather
not yet arrived at the square,
the chairs mostly empty.
She can see the ghost
of someone who used to sit there,
who liked the sun's glare
in her eyes in early morning,
early spring, that hint of heat
a glaze that made the shapes
of her worlds congruent, the mind
a fabric laid over the city,
its details imprinted
like blossoms on silkscreen,
a map she could follow.

THE BODY WANTS
TO SLEEP

It is smart enough to know
what the morning will be:

sodden legs,
eyes that think

they must have been weeping.
But the brain cannot stop

its reckless bird dance,
its strut, shiver

of feathers, wings spread
and beating

like the frenzied
push toward sex

that makes everything whir
and stand still at once.

Nothing could distract it
short of fire sweeping

through the grasses,
even the strawberries aflame.

The moon slides low
through a cloudless sky

like dreams orbiting
the night.

The brain flies wild
above the body it would enter.

EVERY ANGEL IS TERRIBLE

To Radovan Karadzic

On the borders, what is known
on one side sometimes cannot
be said on the other.

More than a decade ago—
two poets, American, in a land
of seams stretched thin,
of languages stitched
into a jacket nobody loved,
nobody wore without shrugging.

By the time a bus eased us
from Dubrovnik,
half asleep, toward Sarajevo,
we'd bathed, untoweled
each other on a balcony
above the turquoise sea.

It didn't matter that our phone
was tapped, the room wired
to earphones somewhere.
We'd hushed our voices
but were amused
that anyone might see
or care. Even when the desk clerk
knew our next destination,
we laughed. Tito was dead.
This was the one free
Communist country.

That last warm night
at the Mad-Maison, we drank
too much pear brandy,
our indiscretions public—
on the terrace, my sheer dress
lifting in the breeze,
the lacing of our legs—
as if we knew

we wouldn't return,
or if by chance we did,
these people
would no longer be there.

Sarajevo gave us
more of ourselves, each other—
in the markets, in churches,
in the ferny graveyard

where you, Radovan, our host, guide,
interpreter, became our friend.
You explained the simple
double tombstones—
head and foot—of the Moslem
graves. Hands on stone,
we measured distances diminishing
between us, among us. Your strong arm
swept the horizon
where minarets paralleled cedars
and everything pointed to heaven.

Sometimes, when love takes root,
we become the tamped-down soil
and the vines. When we stretch our arms,
we are the forest.

At breakfast you spoke of Rilke's angels
while Turkish coffee
slid down our throats
slow and sweet
as the night we'd arrived from.

Later, in the hotel dining room,
a man collapsed, clutching his chest.
You, the good doctor,
ran to the stage with your bag,
checked his eyes, his pulse,
slipped something under his tongue.

Think how we relinquish ourselves
on a continuum—unconscious pain
becoming aches so pleasurable

we cannot keep from sighing.
We cannot explain
except by saying, perhaps,
that bread is being broken
by the soul and the body.

The church of St. Michael
narrow and dark. Figures in gold leaf
brightened the corners, relics
saved from fire. We were in thrall
to your voice, your formal English
deepened to whisper.
You explained the dimensions:
by the sultan's permission,
the church was rebuilt,
exactly as small as before.

In the garden, sunlight
blinds. Eyes closed, we discover
how much we can hear
if we direct ourselves to the hummingbird
above the salvia. Even if we'd never
seen red, red becomes an impatience
of wings.

When you helped us bargain
for the diamond-patterned rugs,
the Turkish merchant stamping his foot
at my low offer, you
were bemused, we thought, then
embarrassed. You told us
a fair price and we paid it
against a backdrop of scarved women
and solemn children sitting on rugs,
skeins of wool, dyed and undyed,
spread around them.

Arms about our shoulders, you steered us
through passages we hadn't found,
narrow streets where gates opened
to rainy courtyards,
green chairs and tables on the cobblestone,

restaurants with plain white rooms
where you read us your poems.

When those untranslated lines
fell like darkness on our ears,
what we understood was of the flesh,
our first preoccupation,
then something we could not have named.
Hands on each other's thighs
under the table, we listened
half to you, half to our own need.

In that slant October light
that follows rain,
it felt as if we were spring,
greening the landscape—

a landscape now caressed by flame,
where air is ash.

Who were you, we ask,
and who are we beneath our words?

The borders change.
We do not know what anything means.

White syllables in every language
drift toward silence.

WATER HAS NO
CONSTANT SHAPE

my student is quoting
Sun-tzu
The Art of War
when I see

the backs of buttons
on my Chinese jacket

characters etched
into the brass
where they would never
be seen

except by the wearer
by chance

the notes do not exceed
five but the changes
of the five notes can
never be fully heard

the colors do not exceed
five but the changes
of the five colors can
never be completely seen

like Surprise Lilies
or camouflaged soldiers
appearing scattered one day
without warning
through the tall grass

the one who excels
at sending forth
the unorthodox
is as inexhaustible
as heaven

as unlimited
as the Yangtze
and Yellow Rivers

so many signs
we do not understand
languages we have
not learned

language of beauty
language of death

what reach an end
and begin again
are the sun and moon

how must the morning sun
appear to a man
dying in a field

moments of light
darting from trees

it might seem
his first glimpse of the world

RETURNING

It must be genetic, proof that the road
is not a series of signs to be deciphered
but a place the mind already knows.
We never can say how we got there,
but find ourselves back where we started,
hearts pizzicato at every missed turn
in a world designed to dissuade us ever
from leaving home.

Once in a country where I
knew neither landscape nor language,
a new friend lent me his car
and waved me off. I arrived
at a walled city, climbed through a maze
of golden streets and rested in a café.
Later, the missing purse—
passport, money, keys. The name
of my friend's village gone like a dream
too many hours after waking. Breathless,

blinded by panic, I ran through that network
of narrow lanes, the cobblestones Braille.
At last—the café. The owner shook her finger,
railed, and handed me the bag I'd left,
everything intact. After that I wound my way
through dusk, through villages I had not passed
to the place I'd begun. I think

it's a kind of grace—like geometry,
where right answers come through paths
we can never retrace—showing we're blessed.
Lost, lost, we cry, but return
like pigeons whose routes are unerring, unearned.

AT DUKE UNIVERSITY
MEDICAL CENTER

My mother in the cylinder
lies still, her small
sandaled feet protruding.
The MRI chugs and clanks and chugs
and then it chimes,
church bells in the distance.
I stop reading to listen.

By now she's forgotten
why she's here, how long
she's been encased,
and where we are.
The church bells stop.
A dental drill begins,
the quickened beat
of a heart magnified
behind it like backup
drums, or water sloshing
iambic against a dock.
An hour has passed.

I wonder if she sleeps,
God cocooned beside her,
if she dreams
she's mummified,
memory restored
and sailing with her soul
to the other side.

The technician's voice,
projected from her booth,
glassed in behind us,
sounds digital
before an impatient knocking—
someone wanting passage—
and a door seems to open
by degrees, squeaking

at each interval.
Half an hour more.

All this will disappear
in the car going home
to South Carolina.
She'll think she's in Wisconsin,
the miles erased
like the decibels
her ears are plugged against.
She'll ask if we're going
to church on Sunday
and what she should wear.

Above the ratcheting of the machine,
I hear the swish of her skirt
forty years ago,
the ghost of a prayer.

WHERE WE HAVE COME

1 *The Solace of Poems*

To discover them
is to link with the unbroken
griefs we name and rename.

The death, by degrees,
of a mother
is a kind of death
of self.

Without a mirror
I see my face,
her mouth pinched;
know, from the inside,
fingers tapping the table,
an almost demure
drop of the head.

This is part of it.

But to see loss
black on white
is to be comforted
a moment
in the early hours,
not left alone
to mourn a mind
dropping its history
like Gretel's bread,
birds swooping behind.

2 *After the Latest Descent*

Slow motion
through the death
that is not
death enough,

room after room
locking, locked, where
creatures caught inside
scratch at windows,
at the light
under doors.

The keys turn, by contrast,
quietly. Something determined
slips down the halls,
listening, as children disappear
in the airless chambers,
then husbands, Christmas
dinners, faces
in frames

until only the snake brain
remains in the stubborn,
irrelevant body.

She is halfway there.
This is minor preparation.

3   *What Does It Matter*

that another old woman goes,
mind first, her words
become less lovely
than whirs of wings at night
in the disturbed bamboo,
a startled rapping against leaves
that takes the heart.

4   *Where We Have Come*

Walking the same
green path, day
after day, we watched a duck
drop an egg, later
ducklings like a yellow fan
on the red-brown water.
This is where we sat,

where I tried to teach us
concentration.

She is moving toward
peace—the first time
in her life, now,
as her brain knots
its fine yarns.
How can it be? At the same time
that something releases,
something like God
enters her. Her laugh
is girlish, full
of delight.

Death is still
a stranger, but
he carries lilacs.

NOT SWANS

I drive toward distant clouds and my mother's dying.
The quickened sky is mercury, it slithers
across the horizon. Against that liquid silence,
a V of birds crosses—sudden and silver.

They tilt, becoming white light as they turn, glitter
like shooting stars arcing slow motion out of the abyss,
not falling.
      Now they look like chips of flint,
the arrow broken.
      I think, This isn't myth—

they are not signs, not souls.
                  Reaching blue
again, they're ordinary ducks or maybe
Canada geese. Veering away they shoot
into the west, too far for my eyes, aching

as they do.

      Never mind what I said
before. Those birds took my breath. I knew what it meant.

I'M WATCHING HER

disappear, the air
takes her body and whoosh—
nothing but white cloud,
blue sky.

I push the clouds back
like a wisp of hair
fallen over one eye—
pretense of clarity.
I know this,
and also the danger.

She is standing
at a clothesline
between sheets so white
they look as if they were meant
to be written on. They flap
wetly: snap—they're dry,
the clothespins fall
into a canvas hamper,
making a soft clack
and another.

Lightning—
a new century.
Look—my skin is silver
one jagged moment
before it's obscured.

FROM *Trinity* (1996)

I

THE GOSPEL ACCORDING TO
MARY MAGDALENE

On the subjects of which we know nothing, we both believe and
disbelieve a hundred times an Hour, which keeps Believing nimble.
—Emily Dickinson

1   *The Casting Out of the Seven Devils*

Lord, I said to him, I sin.
What moves me to answer the flesh

when spirit calls in its light
and singular tones?

A well-made man is never invisible
to me, even beneath heavy cloaks.

Sometimes, as morning gathers toward heat,
a man's arm brushes mine in the market.

Then a bolt shoots through me like lightning,
the scent of earth rising around me.

What is this trembling, why does the wind
itself become dark breath on my skin?

I asked him these things.
I did not tell him that he

made my nights a desert where stars
were so bright they drilled into me

lying alone on the dunes. My kind of longing
was not his command.

I meant to do his bidding, though what he bade
passed through me like music.

Woman, he told me, *I know you well.*
Though devils spin you through lives

you cannot and do not wish in your blood
to forget, they are a gang of thieves

who will, if we don't throw them out,
take the gold and the silver

your heart would leave
on my father's altar. They will strip

your walls bare where now
you delight your wakings with silk.

The rugs piled soft for your bed
will be rolled up and carried away.

These thieves will make you believe
the house of your body is aflame

and take everything
in the name of rescue.

Cast them out, Lord, I prayed.
Let me come to you rich with treasures.

His eyes described my being.
He took me by my shoulders, his hands

lifted me, and I felt the devils depart
all at once, my head in sudden pain

that left me so weak, I fell back
to my knees, weeping.

Mary, he said, so softly
I barely heard him. *Mary*,

as his hands stroked my hair,
as his hands stroked and stroked my hair.

2 *The Anointing*

I arrived at the house of Simon, a Pharisee.
My master sat at his table, red wine

and lamb before him, the fresh meat
steaming, the fragrance of olive oil

a perfume of gold in the air.
I could not help myself, I began

to weep. I knelt before my lord
and let my tears fall, washing his dusty feet

in that overflow of rapture,
then dried them with my hair.

I could not speak, for his presence
stopped my words

as if they were stunned
with drink. I drew a small box

from inside my robe.
Opening its alabaster lid,

I poured ointment over those feet
while even the dove in the window

grew silent. Jesus loved
my penitence first,

then the way my hair fell
to the floor, its weight against his skin.

I kissed my lord's ankles
as if Simon were not in the room,

as if the other guests were not
exchanging glances.

Jesus laid his hand on my hand,
spoke to Simon and the others:

Try to understand, he said.
I have come for her as well.

*My father never
blinded me to beauty.*

*She is a flame whose light
burns whiter now that I am here.*

*And I? Look into my eyes,
black with awakening.*

Even I must learn my way
by trial and touch.

The dove flew to my shoulder.
I felt its body hesitate, the tremolo of wings.

When the men spoke again,
only the voice of Jesus

entered my ear. I did not hear
meaning. It was like my own heart

beating wild, the sea
pulsing in, the tide rising.

3   The Wedding at Cana

I welcomed his mother into my arms.
Still young, she commanded her son

in a voice he sometimes rebuked, but she
would have her say. Though the servants

were mine, she ordered the feast—
goat cooked with mint and pears, spiced breads,

doves wrapped in grape leaves, baked in wine,
figs, an array of honeyed cakes,

and more. She saw to the cloths spread
on tables, hung branches over the doors.

She perfumed the house with incense and cedars,
that fragrance wafting to my room

where a girl brushed my hair,
braided it with lavender. Why was I afraid?

Bridegroom, I wanted to cry, to call him
to me. But he was welcoming guests

from Nazareth and from Capernaum,
from Magdala, my village, and from Gennesaret.

There were those who traveled even from Hebron
and Bethlehem, and from Arimathea.

When I came out, some of the faces turned dark,
like poplar leaves in sudden wind.

So many, I could not recognize friends.
Bodies pressed back, making a path

for me through my house, now unfamiliar
as a foreign temple. But he took my hand,

and when the vows were said, my heart lifted
and was glad. Then his mother whispered

that the wine was nearly gone.
She called the servants. Jesus said,

Fill all the jars with water. When
they returned it was wine.

Love, I said to him, I was water,
flowing over banks, flooding fields

already wet from too much rain.
You contained me. You changed me.

Which is the greater miracle?
More gently than I had heard her,

his mother answered: He is the vine.
This is all we must remember.

4 *The Crucifixion*

I was afraid. My fear was so great
the doves would not come to me,

though I stood in a circle of crumbs,
arms extended, hands filled with bread.

I did not go into the hall
where the men ate their last feast together.

My lord had instructed me to prepare the tomb,
to lay clean cloths on a boulder,

to leave a jug of water there.
Trust my heart, he said.

It has been tested.
My father wishes me to die

and not to die.
Each morning I give myself

to the dust of the road,
each night to the dark and to you

whose lips chart
my still unbroken flesh.

It is written, he said,
his pulse changing. *I must go.*

That night I watched the moon
cross over the garden,

the moon with its placid
face, gliding as if through water,

as if it were breathing through water.
I wanted to absorb its white, cast

into the trees like hope,
or to be absorbed.

When I was with him, I believed.
My heart's wings grew quiet. But away

from his hungry body, that body singing
its clear, sharp note into the cedars,

I lost faith in the fragile plan.
There in Gethsemane, I tried to pray.

Nothing. Nothing but the rustling
of leaves, then a cloud racing to obscure

the moon, so that the garden fell
into heavy shadow, animals stalked

the paths. A wind came up fast.
Limbs torn from the olive trees

were cast on the ground. I ran, shaken,
to my brother's house. When Jesus entered

my chamber late with a lamp, I saw the bones
in his face, the wells under his eyes.

We did not speak.
All night, we were one voice.

I could not watch them scourge him,
though I heard the lashes

split the parched air,
heard the tearing of his skin.

I could not follow close
as he staggered under the weight

on his bloodied back.
From a distance, I saw him stumble.

Lord, Lord, I cried, what will become of us?
I was ashamed,

thinking of myself. I stood at the edge
of the crowd as they drove the nails.

Too far away to hear his groans, yet
they filled my throat, seemed wrenched

from my mouth. When the cross was raised,
I fell to the ground, lay there, I think, for hours,

while the crowd, restless, drank wine from skins,
stepped over me, laughing.

I could not urge my spirit
or my eyes to rise.

At last, a shout went up. I raised my head,
saw a cup lifted to his lips.

Not vinegar, as some reported later,
but something to make him sleep

a drowning sleep, a sleep
so close to death he'd feel

the water closing over him,
his breath dissolving

under waves of dream.
Oh, that he might survive—

but if the measure were wrong, the dream
would end, and—more mercifully—he'd die.

My love's head fell forward.
It was over.

They took him down. I struggled up.
Someone helped me walk.

After that, I don't remember.
In my brother's house, I slept

until he woke me. Go, he said. Jesus is waiting.
I went to the tomb, my heart beating double.

I waited until the stone rolled back. Two men
in white attended him, two Essenes. They motioned me

to come in. My kisses
were balm, my lord said, and would renew him.

I pressed my mouth to his mouth,
to his eyelids, then to his wounds.

His mother came in, and other women.
We carried him out into the sun,

which fell in rings
all around him.

5   *The Flight into Gaul*

In my brother's house we passed an anxious week.
The two Essenes stayed,

their white robes flowing quiet
through the rooms. They took turns standing watch

outside his door, those guardian angels. The rest
of us—me, his mother Mary, and my brother—

sat *shiva*. When guests came,
grief was not hard to feign in our exhaustion

and our fear. When we were alone, we gathered
grapes, salted lamb, put by a few clean robes.

From time to time, my husband woke in fever,
not himself, shouting curses

mixed with prayers. He implored—
How many chambers

must I enter, Father?
The wolves of darkness devour me!

What flies in at the window?
What beats its black body against the walls?

What drums against the air?
He covered his ears

against what he heard,
and I could not persuade him

of the silence. At last his brow
grew cool again, he asked for water.

On the day the Essenes proclaimed him well
enough to travel, we filled the skins

with water, packed bread and blankets.
By camel, by starlight, we traveled

to the sea, where my brother had arranged
our passage. The boatman did not know us,

thought us poor, glad to trade a simple fare
for the camels. He told us to be patient

while he led them
to a stable in the distance.

Half a day we wasted, waiting for that man
to amble back. None of us was calm.

Jesus stayed in the shadows, watched the sky,
his eyes ringed dark. I paced

beneath the plane trees,
keeping watch for passersby who might recognize

my lord. By noon, the air was still.
No leaf shimmered green to silver.

The few clouds maintained
their languid shapes. I fed my husband raisins.

His mother frowned when he took my fingers
in his mouth. I felt a shiver in my womb.

By then, the water was so calm
I could see my face reflected, swollen.

At last, my brother pushed us off,
the craft heavy with the five of us.

The boatman, old enough to be my father,
rowed with the strength of two young men.

Our destination was Narbonne, a settlement
of Jews where we might live.

6   The Branching

Between the pains, I remembered
the words of my lord:

The body, miraculous, rises
on blue wings, rises

out of agony and stupor so quickly
it's hard to remember the dark

paths of its going. It rises
shivering, then warms to stillness.

The body does not believe
in words, but in updrafts of air,

impossible transformations,
sun surrounding it, the whole skin shining.

Between the pains, I panted these words
and other litanies: Abraham was father

to Isaac, who was father to Jacob,
who was father to Judas.

I said the names, the charms
of the names, up to Matthan, who was father

to Jacob, who was father to Joseph,
the husband of Mary

of whom was born Jesus the Nazarene,
my husband, who came to be called Christ.

And Jesus, I murmured, is father to the child
who will be born here

in the city of Narbonne, in Gaul,
of me, Mary the Magdalene.

Lord, I cried to my husband, I am riven,
I will be delivered not of devils now but of the son

of the son of kings. Flesh is made holy
in us. Once more and once more I cried

as the pains came faster. Mary
his mother laid cool cloths on my brow.

Let us follow rivers back to their source, I whispered.
Let us cross white mountains into paradise,

into the promised land of the spirit.
Jesus prayed outside the room. He heard,

he listened to my words, my pleas.
He said, *Yes, we will go*

inland. We will enter new lands,
my kingdom will be vast, unending.

When it was finished, I rested, I slept.
I saw my image carved

in marble, with a child.
I dreamed my husband's mouth

at my breast, woke to the infant Benjamin
suckling, the vine branching, the changed world.

II

FROM LETTERS BACK

God Responds to Emily Dickinson

Unless we become as Rogues, we cannot enter the kingdom of heaven.
—Emily Dickinson, in a letter to Dr. Holland

⤸

In school you lean over a microscope,
astonished by revelations
under glass, such minute clarity
controlled.

I tell you, child, there is more power
in the way your mind brings matter
into focus and recombines the elements,
more beauty infused in the world
by your naked eye.

You think you want congruence,
our imaginations closer
than the rings of Saturn,
yours just enclosed in mine.

Let it be enough that a few things
are predictable. You know
when you can peaches
your mother's mood
becomes a wren.

Let your will resist me,
the future be the sky you'll map,
heaven visible like stars
when they are.

⤸

What do you think it means
that you dream of your father's house
flooding, that solid brick lifted

from its moorings, the whole
house floating west, toward the center
of Amherst? I know it puzzles you
that sometimes you are inside
looking down the stairs to the hall
where nobody hears you calling
for Vinnie, who may be trapped
in the kitchen. You watch in fascination
as your mother's prize side table
floats toward the door and out,
as the carpets lift from the floors,
promising next to be airborne.
Sometimes you're walking back
from shopping in the village
when you see the house
coming toward you, its grace not lost
in its drift from one side
of the watery street to the other.
Your father in the doorway
waves as if you were a guest
coming late for dinner, as if it's he
who's moving toward an unfathomed future.
Either way, you are not frightened.
And when you wake, you feel
that you know what the others
don't know, though you cannot
explain it. Let me tell you
this much: when in the morning
you put a finger into the garden's
April soil, the earth
will be soft and damp. You'll soon
name its richness desire.

Now your mother sleeps while you
gather the minutes between one form
of tending and another
to write prayers. Your father
away again, she is all yours,
burden and pleasure, like a garden.

You wonder how men imagine the world—
the invisible polishing of furniture,
the way meals appear,
loaves and fishes to be blessed.
You, ghostlike, deliberately
not holy, float to your mother's room
with a tray, hoping he'll ask
after your health on his return.
Sometimes I fear you listen for my voice
in his: distracted, not knowing
what he does not want to hear.

       ↫

You know the trees sing differently
for you, full of minor chords.
It's true, most who pass under that shelf
of elms hear something that doesn't rhyme
but blends to a plain sweetness.

There is less to quicken the pulse
in other people's nights
than in your noons, when everything turns
toward imbalance. What I love is that

you love that tilt, however you lament,
and fill it with a consequence the others miss—
and that you hear dissonance
under the cardinal's call.

       ↫

Look at you. A careless stranger
or the postman might think you mad,
staring into the clover, your hair
loose around your shoulders.
You forget yourself. Oh, I tolerate
too much impudence, the way you whirl
around me as if I were a canna
and you a hummingbird, quick
and innocent as earliest Eden.
There is history still
to be made. Try to remember

that even as your eyes fail,
my sight penetrates each particle
of the earth, each trumpet vine
and snail, each parlor where a soul,
in its pride, thinks itself alone.

         ↩

What do you tell yourself
when dreams skitter away
like rabbits, any gesture
enough to set them running?

You say you listen for me
later in the garden,
sometimes hear
the whisper of the dill,
but not my voice.

Today I came before first light
to sit with you, watching
your closed eyes flutter.
What passed through you then
was a procession. I was one
of the mourners, disguised,
who held out his hand.
You kept your head down,
did not look at my face
but put coins in my palm
as if I were the beggar.

         ↩

Why, when I speak to myself,
do I so often think of you?
You've hardly seen the world,
while I contain it. And yet
when my net flies out, settles
in a hush over the river,
you're the one who never
feels trapped, who knows
how to weave
in and out of that mesh.

I like having you on the earth,
a reminder that what I give there,
so often misconstrued, is felt
in one who could not be my wife
or sister, but walks
the labyrinth of my love
as if she had a map.

⁓

I know it is meant for me,
this new sign of impatience—
ripping up the mint and the daisies,
suddenly hating prolixity
and how the seasons
increase their demands.
So today you court endings again.

You think you listen for me,
but it's your own will
you hear. It pounds in your ears
like rain against rock.
It reminds you that you choose,
over and over, to till
one plot, small, obdurate.

⁓

Today someone asks you
to define the soul.
It is what remains, you say,
when strength has left
the arms, when the muscles
are too fatigued to remember
their old grace.
It is what remains,
though no one can guarantee
that its wings are not like arms.
No one can say for certain
that it will carry itself
out the doors of the body
and back to its home.

It is a sparrow, you say,
sometimes weighted with ice.

But I tell you, it is not
a sparrow. The soul is a hawk.
It makes shadows ripple over
the earth. It writes boldly
against the light, its form solid
in what you claim is flimsy air.

      ∽

You think I am never alone.
In one sense it's true—
the world, so much a part
of me, so much my own,
cannot allow my absence.

I sometimes stand back, away,
but it's as if you, dreaming,
had set yourself down
in the South.

Waking, you'd be blinded by dogwood
brushing whole branches
against your window.

Human voices might drift
somewhere beyond or behind you,
but your mind would be
so filled with white,
you'd hear and not hear them.

In fact, this is aloneness
having nothing to do
with geography.

When you are most yourself,
which is to say, most estranged,
I am there, in the room,
equally removed.

III

FROM IN THE ABIDING DARK

Oh, Sir, may one eat of hell fire with impunity here?
>—Emily Dickinson's remark at a dinner
>where flaming plum pudding was served

She prayed, and her prayer was monstrous because in it there was no
margin left for damnation or forgiveness, for praise or for blame—those
who cannot conceive a bargain cannot be saved or damned.
>—Djuna Barnes, *Nightwood*

Every man and every artist, whether he is Nietzsche or Cézanne, climbs
each step in the tower of his perfection by fighting his duende, not his
angel, as has been said, nor his muse. This distinction is fundamental, at
the very root of the work.
>—Federico García Lorca

1

We know that everything comes down to choice.
One night I find myself at a party,
critics yelling at each other, ice

rattling in their glasses like sabers—an arty
gathering, all the duels safely verbal.
I do not join any argument. My body

becomes the antagonist: I hear there's a ball
being held downstairs. "You can't go there,"
one of the critics says. "Only men are allowed."

He bars the door. The others stare
in disapproval as I slip past the barrier
of his arms. I descend the stairs

into a room where women are carried
naked into other rooms and to shadowed corners,
where couples are coupling everywhere

I look: women embrace women, men fornicate
with anyone in reach. The light is smoky,
someone makes a joke. The word *foreigners*

hovers on a sneer. Someone pokes
me in the ribs. I see a raised footbridge
and begin to cross, the clouds already broken

up and lifting, the air brighter, richer.
I breathe deep, watch the light flow
around me. Even the temperature shifts,

cooler, yet it feels as if the sun had shone
there always. Along a narrow hall,
scenes of women dancing are frescoed

the whole white length of the wall.
"Did you paint this?" I ask a woman
suddenly there, her filmy dress and shawl

also like a dancer's. "It's in the wind's hand,"
she laughs, beckoning me to follow.
She takes me to another room, where music stands

are punctuation marks against the yellow
chairs, the pine-green rug.
Music is the subject. "Do you allow

strangers?" I ask timidly. A woman shrugs,
smiles, pulls me into her group.
They stand in a circle discussing Wagner

and *The Ring*. Carol is among them, her harp
propped beside her. I say, "I believe
I've been here before." She starts

playing, the sound of October leaves
swirling and falling. She nods. "The furniture's
been changed," she says. The others retrieve

their instruments and go. From above, a lecture
by one of the critics grows loud. "The quality
of an artist's work," he shouts, "can be measured

by the quality of the bargain he
makes with the devil." Outside, the ensemble
is tuning up. Someone strikes a key.

. . . .

3

Saturday mornings I biked to Mrs. Mann's,
nearly always late for piano lessons.
Stout and saintly, my teacher never rapped hands

with a ruler, rarely chastened
with the metronome. I felt little shame for cheating
on my practice time. What I chose to listen

to and play were not the pieces
she assigned, cheerful melodies
evoking lacy dawns; I wanted icy evenings,

northern landscapes, threnodies
where every note fell labored, dark runs
and minor chords—tunes with more black keys

than my skills could navigate. I pumped
the loud pedal, blurred errors blissfully,
all *Sturm und Drang*, all thunder.

On the radio one Sunday, Mozart's *Dissonant
Quartet*. The introduction was all I needed.
I danced. From then on I insisted

all my music had to be diaphony,
until my teacher lost her famous patience.
When my parents let me quit, I'd succeeded.

Distance and time say it wasn't just laziness
and perversity. Like Tartini, I've dreamed
the devil in my chamber, curtains ablaze,

violins. He's not entirely what he seems
in paintings and the myths. Yes, passionate—
his cape and grin flamboyant. Yes, a fiend

who can entice a mother to murder her innocent
child, a man to fire a pistol into a crowd.
But what's less often seen is his intense

delight in what we do in the flood
of his love. There is another Angelus
that calls. We hear the loud

chime of its bell, a tritone Diabolus
in Musica. Trust what comes from below,
it peals. It speaks to me. It speaks to us.

4

How do we glide into our knowing?
What happens when we imagine the dust
we'll become? Can anything slow our dying?

A man lunches in a bright café, casting lustful
glances at the next table's lamb
and potatoes au gratin, at the woman who must

be dreaming there in the corner, her hands
clasped in her lap, head tilted
as if she listens to wind over sand

in some distant country, memory half silted
over. Somehow he already knows
that this is what their lives will be built

on. He imagines now that wherever they go
the past will live between them, sometimes
a cloud, sometimes a glittering show

that plays, with variations, in his mind,
a theater of reds and blacks. He is confident
that this is it: the world is not always kind,

but it's what we have—nothing radiant
waits on the other side. He's decided to garner
all possible joys, to plan the events

of his continuing, not to squander
the years ahead. He speaks to her.
And so it begins. Late, the two of them meander

out and down the vacant, narrow street. He burns
to say what it's too soon to speak of.
It *can* happen like this, though he's learned

no one trusts a man's sudden intentions in love.
Even he has always believed it's mostly glands,
no bolt of lightning, certainly, from above.

Whatever intuition is, it stands
in the shadows, rarely speaks in a man's voice,
we think. How much we fail to understand.

5

Are you the dreamer in the café? If so, what choice
do you have? Swept by events, by his ardent
promises, will you see this as fate? If there's a price,

when will you know it? Let's say you consent
to a voyage. You stop at a fishing village,
salt-battered houses, stores. There's been an accident.

A drowned girl has been brought in on a skiff.
She lies on the shore, the strands of her hair spread
in a sandy halo, her body rigid.

A crowd has gathered. Your lover buys bread
to feed the gulls. You want to find out
who she was, who loved her, what she said

before she left. He tells you this happens about
once a month. For people who live by the sea
and know better, he says, they're inclined to flout

safety. Look at their eyes. They're eager
to cast those slim bodies into the deep.
Sad, he says, but how it will always be

in these parts. You feel a sudden need to sleep.
He arranges your hair on the pillow, a fan.
In the morning, he brings coffee steeped

long, strong enough to wash the sand
from your eyes. By the time
you come home, you're wearing a wedding band.

And after that? It's true that we find
what we need. A darkness will prevail
in the evenings, when the restless mind

travels. You'll pick up a book, put it down, fail
to find the tape you want, play Robert Johnson,
then Paganini. Eyes closed, you'll see a plumed tail.

. . . .

8

Who is our brother? Who hears
us when we cry? Or when our child
cries? More to the point, the child dearest

to me, my own, the son whose wildness
as a boy, long-haired and drug-inflamed,
was not an ordinary break from the island

of the family, rebellion I could blame
on culture, the adolescent rage
that's like a fever. No, this was a maimed

child, whose mother came of age
too late, trading him for other loves and poems,
uncertain Art, a word-woven cage

of reds and blues she'd call her home,
inviting music in, and certain men.
This was my bargain. It left my only

child to wander west, to mend
as he could. All was not well.
Now he builds a house, sends

snapshots of it rising board by board. He sells
his labor cheap, dreams of making sculpture,
of re-creating himself. What do I tell

him? What do I tell myself? Can I nurture
him now that *he* is the age of Jesus at his death?
What does it mean, what conjecture

might connect the pieces? I read of the Earth,
the speculations of philosophers and physicists
about the stars, our place, the search

revealing order. Can a leaf, an eye, be chance? We insist
that it can, it is. And yet the odds deny
this cooled and rhymed universe. What if I stop resisting

that vast intelligence? How should I ally
myself? And what of chaos, that fiery friend
of artists? Does one truth make a lie

of another? Who's at the heart of us? What bends
like steel to belief? How do we make
ourselves artists, and to what end?

The sky explodes with light, and the ache
begins. I dream that my son makes sculpture,
weeping bronze heads, abstractions of wood and paper.

9

When my friend Moni is hired by an austere
American to sculpt Lucifer's image in marble and granite,
he thinks of Drac (Moni is Romanian). His demon appears

to him, speaks his native tongue. A composite
spirit emerges—full, round breast on one side, penis
on the other, gorgeous plumed tail. It

stands now, all three tons, on the terrace
of a villa above Limoux, not far from Rennes-
le-Château. I try to catch a glimpse of the cultists

who live there. I take photos of Moni and his friend
as they install the piece, and of the gardens—purples
and reds, herbs—everything meticulously tended.

In the front the view is a grove of apple
trees and rooftops, the valley below
in mist. Off to the right a steeple

and the cemetery, huge silvery crosses a stone's throw
from the street. Moni welds the base
at the devil's feet. Sparks glow

in the air for minutes, rain into his face
and the devil's. Eyes unmasked, I'm entranced
by the light they make.

Later, on the radio, *Anitra's Dance*. Shall I dance
on the graves of my enemies? I wanted to say
Let me not, but the thought came out backward.

I wake with such urgency these days.
Music conspires again with dreams—
I watch a man and woman waltzing lazily

above the traffic, balanced on a beam
while construction workers pay no
attention, thinking, perhaps, the sweetness

on the air is accident. Liszt's *Consolation*
drifts from a window ten stories up—
someone is practicing, repeats a phrase, slow.

J'ACHÈVE CE DAEMON DE GARDIEN À MIDI POMMES
BLEUES. (I DISPATCH THIS GUARDIAN DEMON AT NOON BLUE APPLES.)
Once more, Ste. Magdalen, a cryptic document. Light comes

through the stained glass at the south end stippled
so that at a certain hour, midday, a tree
ripples into focus, apples ripen red except

for three. Those three stay blue. Stevens's
blue guitar is strummed now by a demon who accompanies
a choir composed of deities

from everywhere. They sing off-key.
They hum Sibelius. They laugh together wildly.
They comfort me.

NOTE: There are a number of mysteries associated with the village of Rennes-le-
Château in the French Pyrenees. The Church of Ste. Magdalen there is a bizarre
concoction of architectural and artistic puzzles, a result of its restoration in the
nineteenth century by the abbé Saunère, who had come into unexplained riches.
Images of the devil abound—in the church itself and in and around the village,
which is believed by many to be the final resting place of Mary Magdalene, who
according to legend was married to Jesus and bore his children. Some recent
studies by scholars of the Dead Sea Scrolls seem to bear out the essential elements
in the legend.

From *Everything Winged Must Be Dreaming*
(1993)

THE MAP OF IMAGINED
GEOGRAPHY

One 16th century map of the world
is remarkably accurate,
latitude and longitude somehow
divined, the cartographer inspired,
like a blind man who feels his way
through any universe, outlines of ideas
imprinted in his fingertips. Angel faces
blow the winds of the world from the margins,
three dark mouths from the south, nine
white ones, lips puckered as for kisses,
warm breath, cold breath, puffs
of cumulus clouds surrounding each
disembodied head. Australia is a vacancy
smooth as drugged sleep,
and North America blurs to a dream.

In the Bar Rossi this morning
a man tells me he nearly died on Friday,
his car a tangle of steel and blood.
His mother weeps. His father
shakes his head, orders cappuccino
for celebration. A dark-eyed woman,
their friend, translates the contours
of two Italian lakes, and the way streets
intersect the town, into slow words
they think they can follow. The man
who feels resurrected, whose face
is swollen, bruised, remembers
nothing of his trajectory,
only light smashing into his eyes
like something he might have seen
in a movie, and an explosion
of sound he thought was his soul.
He could not trace
his way back to the road
but envisions the region as time

when absence filled him like the freezing
lake, a silver territory his mind
swam in, arms flailing, eyes open,
seeing nothing. He emerged
two days ago after wandering the depths
where invisible mountains
rise and shift and change, by stages,
the visible world. On another map
they'd be radiant red patches lifting
toward the surface while iridescent blues
at the edges sink, the earth's floor
dropping and dropping. Today,
dawn arrives from the definition
of the valley where he's learned
to look for it, where it will be tomorrow.

RAINY MORNING IN PUIVERT

The sky as thunder rattles the distance
is a blue that, were it paint
on canvas, would be garish, a teal fog
obscuring the Pyrenees, whose hazy
outline can scarcely be seen,
like a dream you're calling
into consciousness.

Our neighbor, Odette, recently widowed,
fears thunderstorms. She keeps
shutters closed on a day like this,
wanders from one small room to another
thinking of Paul. Too early for me
to go over, and by the time
it's a proper hour, rain will slash
across the road. Is this an excuse?

I love lightning from enough distance,
the whole sky brilliantly open
and then dissolving darkly
back into itself, like something human,
a love affair, then love gone wrong.

"Married over fifty years," she said.
That's our goal. To wake together,
some part of one body touching
the other, listening to rain
on a tile roof, the faint fragrance
of woodsmoke.

No reason to go out.
Everything's closed on Mondays.
I'll watch the sky gradually change,
the Cathar château's ruined tower
emerge from mist the way history
asserts itself here—
insistent as all beauty.

Only Lascale, a smaller village
up the road, wants to let the past go.
Burned by the Germans, everyone killed,
now its symmetrical new tile look
could be any suburb of Carcassonne.

Here, everything's old. This tiny house
had a huge carved stone set into a wall.
From when the château began to crumble,
late 15th century? Nobody knows.
There's a shape on the left
like a Celtic clover. On the right,
a sand-dollar figure, a small
heart above, the whole encased
in a large one. The world's heaviest
valentine, we joke. We had it removed
from its hidden corner to rest
on the wide pine boards
in front of the bed. Perhaps it was
a marriage gift, someone said—
two symbols the crests of families,
the heart above and the heart around
meanings that never alter.
So *logique* we believe it.
And want to. We started
our marriage here, two years ago.

The rain has stopped.
A white cloud rises so fast
in the distance, I think of the bomb.
But of course not. Already
it diffuses, is shaped by a subtle
wind, ascends, begins to join
the pale clean sky
swallows are circling again.

HOW SEEM BEDEVILED BE

On the marriage of Elsie and Wallace Stevens

She was Bo-Peep, bedazzling him
with eyelet pinafores
and almond petit fours.

Be ribboned, he said, let daisies
undulate through your yellow hair
like the hair Yeats claimed

was reason enough for reason
to fly. Blond curls,
billowing, bound him,

gold threads wound
round his heart like braid.
She half-believed, and the letters

rained. They spilled through the roof
of Reading nights, words
slipping their wet way

into her bed,
so that her sleep rolled
with sounds still round

on her tongue as they came
from him. And there were
rainbows on her skin.

The indigo of incidents he sent
was lavender to her loneliness.
She walked the days away,

her adopted name away, on paths
he said were bent to fit
her silken feet, poor indolent Peep.

Poor princess.
Her nights were a cathedral built
to hold the soul he thought

was his, wrought a different
way, perhaps, but sister somehow
to his own. Hardly a kiss

had passed their lips, an occasional
dove, its feathers brushing
sweet as a breeze fresh

from the lush *printemps.*
She teased, and he,
tentative, testy, whispered

of cleaving, chastity, chill.
On the porch swing, under
her mother's nervous eye—

the knowing, uphaphazard eye
she cast on preachers,
poachers, pillars

of the community, they rocked,
she sang a lullaby.
Years passed like this, in sometime

bliss. But mostly she grew tired.
The words got thin as autumn grass,
the months rolled on in carriages

whose passengers they rarely were.
Patience, he said, was the fullest
word, the plumpest bird to watch

display its plumage—slow—
an opening that the peacock knew
and he had come to know.

When the woods came white again
the fifth time round, he gave
his pledge. A secret to be closeted

till pink proclaimed ascendency
(the secret, of course,
from his family).

The choirs didn't sing the solemn day
he carried her over the estuary
into summer. She feared her voice

might never touch that inner string
he plucked himself, to set
his spirit humming.

What if she'd found another man,
a simpler friend, a lover
who would look at a sea and see a sea,

who'd have looked at her and seen Elsie—
no angel of necessity
or figment of reality.

She might have found fair words herself.
Might have turned the burnished sky
into a sign of ecstasy, might have

allowed her mind to glide
into the embrace of buoys
drifting in Miami's bay.

Instead, the giant settled her
in a silent house, saving words
for the prayers

he made—and only made—on paper.
Oh, it was a silvery cage,
to be sure and sure.

Then he become the mountain king,
and on certain nights of their middle age,
an alabaster avalanche.

She was the rock he fell against.

ETIAM PECCATA

On the liaison of Roza Scribor-Rylska and Paul Claudel

For Carol Pharr

> In my arms I have held the human star.
> —Paul Claudel, "L'Esprit et l'Eau"

October, 1900

He falls even faster
than I do, so that when we're both
underwater, he looks surprised,
those great blue eyes open, blinking,
while I dive between his legs,
mermaid, fish, and grasp him
by the waist. Then he's there,
he's with me, and it's
as if there were no husband, sons,
calling from shore in voices
too muffled to hear. We twist
and turn under the waves,
lightning zigzagging
tumultuous water.
We're a ballet, attuned
as mirror images,
blond hair swirling round our heads.
Haloes, Paul says through bubbles,
laughing.

1901

Rosalie, he says. Rosalia, Rosa,
moj kotku, my kitten.
Roza's my name. But I'll be
his Rosalie here, anywhere.
China's so vast, we can be lost
together. Even in Foutcheau—
so many golden rooms in the Consulat,
when the children call from their sleep
I can't hear them. Rosa, he says,

taking my breast in his mouth,
my breasts still full, not
drooping yet from the babies.
White as the sun, he says,
when you look long enough into it,
sun on the ocean's horizon.
Isolde, he says.

1902

In my bed, in my gilded room,
he is the sun and the moon.
I didn't imagine those hands
so capable. You are not handsome,
I said to him once. He laughed,
his hands white birds in the air.
That was before. Now
he doesn't laugh, but slips
them under me, pulls me hard
against him, sometimes weeping.
Your eyes are oceans, I say,
and he doesn't smile,
but closes them, reaches
for me, runs his hands over my body
as if he were searching for something
not there. I turn to those hands.

1903

Sinners, he calls us.
He speaks my husband's name
in the middle of love,
rolls away before the rapture can come
to take us out of ourselves
so that we hover somewhere
above our bodies, the room
insubstantial as air.

I am learning to write
Chinese characters.
The one that means love is too complex,

but here is "to be together, to fit"— 共同一致
and here is "bewitch"— 使着迷
I give them to Paul,
who tells me to learn
the figure for God.
I do— 上帝
He is not satisfied,
not even pleased.
Now when he parts my legs
in the darkness,
I fear for the end.
The sounds escaping from him
are growls, like pain.
He says it's his soul slipping away.

I take my sons out to the garden.
They feed the swallows
that swoop almost into their laps
for the bread.
My sons are like birds themselves,
small-boned like their father.
I think of their father, who chose
the jungle, a dangerous
mission for money,
how he installed me with Paul
and went whistling away.

Paul spends hours in the chapel.
He wants to do penance,
but can't, for I'm in an upstairs
bedroom, humming, and he feels
himself pulled in, he says.
He says I'm making him do this.
I say nothing as he unbuttons
my dress, puts his shaking hands
on my breasts, and pushes me
onto the bed.

1904

What is the soul, I ask him,
that it should make such demands?
Woman, he tells me, you are
the spirit's fever, you raise
the temperature until
it dies, delirious, thirsty.
When I tell him I have fever
myself, he leaves the room.

The Chinese doctor has hands
like a woman's, gentle and lithe
as lilies. I'm pregnant,
he tells us. Paul's face
is porcelain. And then it cracks.
I pack my valises. Trembling
with calm, I tell Paul,
Because you believe you need to choose,
you must choose God. I know
you now. You think your body
is the enemy—and mine. You think
of our flesh as having made pacts,
bargains you can't control.

I'm surprised when he yells at me:
No, it's too late!
He orders the cook to make quail
he'd imported from France,
and brings out one of the hoarded
Saint-Emilions. He laughs,
but the sound is like coughing.
I'm already lost, he says.
Don't go.

But I'm gone. And I take
such a circuitous route,
he can't follow: Japan,
San Francisco, New York.
I'm in Belgium now, where winter
makes hard white tracks
on my heart.

He's learned where I am
and writes letters so fat
I wonder what else he must do
with his days. No need to open
or read them. I know
what they say.

The baby is growing large
inside me, my breasts
meet my belly. I'm carrying
high this time. Can it mean
a girl? A pain begins above
my right hip, moves around
my back to the left, where
it settles drunkenly in,
close to the baby.

January 22, 1905

It *is* a girl. An easier birth
than the others, easier
than I'd prepared for,
the sheets hardly bloody.
My sister says I'm blessed,
that when the baby came,
her brilliant blue eyes
were already open. Still opaque,
they look like the paper
Paul used to wrap crystal beads—
a gift once, for me.
I'll call her Louise,
after Paul's mother.

April 1905

My sister warns me
he's coming here.
We pack again, uneasily.
I dream of his weight
the whole length of my body,
dream the moment we'd both

become weightless, the closest
I've been to the flight
of the soul. Blasphemy,
I think sadly.
It's what he'd say.
My arms shiver, even filled
with the warmth of Louise.

I leave a medal of Saint Benoit
on the bed for him to find,
an old silver medal
I bought in a shop near here.
I liked the pattern of tarnish,
the saint's eyes dark, staring
into what only he sees.
Poverty. Chastity. Obedience.

September 1905

Francis, my husband, is dead.
The telegram came from Cochin China
today. It's what he wanted—to die
with the calls of exotic birds
in his ears.
The boys will be sad, though all
they remember is the day he left them
with kisses and sacks of hard candy.
Am I sad? My heart feels
hollow, as if a man could walk
into it, tap on the walls,
and get nothing but echo.

Paul has learned of my husband's death.
He says now I'll return,
we can marry, can sanctify flesh,
candles filling the chapel,
their smoke carrying sin away.

My answer is No.
He believed his soul was the prize,
that his God and I were engaged

in immortal combat.
Would he marry the devil?

1910

My new husband, whose hair
shines black as a crow's
bright wing under moonlight,
is nothing like Paul.
A good man who thinks
the world is simple, and I
its sapphire center. More babies.
I chose this, I think,
and I choose it each day
I open my eyes
to the velvet drapes
he pulls slowly back
to reveal the room
washed in whiteness.
So why do I weep
at a Chinese teapot
in any store window?
Louise slaps her tiny sister
and I feel my cheek redden.
I flush at a word or a gesture
that's hers, that's her father's.
He's married too. A wife
he let God choose,
and who serves him.

1920

I follow his journeys. I have
fastened a map of America
to my dressing-room mirror, and trace
his movements in ink.
His poems are in every
librairie window.
God is his shadow, it seems,
or he the shadow of God

trying to stand in full sunlight.
I buy his books,
their covers plain as a priest's
summer mantle. Each
a reproach.
The poems do not enter me
whole, but in fragments,
like slivers of glass.
When I turn in my sleep
toward my husband,
pain wakes me, pain
not of the flesh, yet rooted
so deep in the body
its source seems everywhere.

1930

It doesn't end.
I dream the sound of his breathing
and wake to his name.
I can hardly pick up *Le Monde*
without seeing that face, grown full,
the photographs always in profile,
so that he seems to be looking
away.

I think of my pride,
how when I left I thought of myself
as a sailboat,
defying the winds,
my small sails filling,
destination unknown.
Now I'm more like a kite
caught in one updraft
after another.
A child, he'd tell me.
You think like a child.
His voice would be rueful,
his mouth trapped
between passion and frown.

1948

The premiere of *Partage de Midi*.
I slip into the Odeon alone,
sit far in the back, discover
his play is our lives, astounding
revision: the carriage of love
rushed him toward Hades
(that much always his truth)
but then—gone—somehow
I became Beatrice,
flicked silver reins, swept
his chariot to heaven.
Transformed to an angel of God,
I was made for one purpose—
to lead him to salvation.

Elixir of lies!

All these years,
in his mind that must carve everything
to a shape that fits squares
like a chessboard
(how could I have forgotten?),
we have been whittled to figures
who move only where he puts them.
I stand, a pawn
in his God's bewildering light,
arms raised in a benediction.
No! I cry into the theater,
my words lost in applause—
I am who I am!

1950

I lead my life. Each Sunday
my children bring their children
to my house. We no longer talk
of the war. When we speak of the past
it's to reminisce—the winter
of no snow, but ice that hung

in intricate constellations
at all the windows,
delicate slips of light
snapping under sun—
or of trips to Spain
when they were young,
expanses of white sand beach
stretched the length of their memories.

The youngest granddaughter is another
Louise, her hair fair as Paul's,
her frown-wrinkle already his.
I loosen the ribbons in her curls, take her
to the Luxembourg Gardens. Somber,
she pulls her blue boat on the pond
in a single direction, clockwise.
Today, when his name drifts
across the small waves on a wind,
nothing in me takes wing.

INVENTING MY PARENTS

After Edward Hopper's *Nighthawks*, 1942

They sit in the bright café,
discussing Hemingway and how
this war will change them.
Sinclair Lewis's name comes up,
and Kay Boyle's, and then Fitzgerald's.
They disagree about the American Dream.
My mother, her bare arms
silver under fluorescent lights,
says she imagines it a hawk
flying over, its shadow sweeping
every town. Their coffee's getting cold
but they hardly notice. My mother's face
is lit by ideas. My father's gestures
are a Frenchman's. When he concedes
a point, he shrugs, an elaborate lift
of the shoulders, his hands and smile
declaring an open mind.

I am five months old, at home with a sitter
this August night when the air outside
is warm as a bath. They decide,
though the car is parked nearby,
to walk the few blocks home, savoring
the fragrant night, their being alone together.
As they go out the door, he's reciting
Donne's "Canonization": "For God's sake
hold your tongue, and let me love,"
and she's laughing, light
as summer rain when it begins.

HAPPINESS: THE FORBIDDEN SUBJECT

Is it because, longing for it,
so many have ripped up their husbands'
glossy photos, carried their wives'
suitcases to cars, everyone crying
as the Chevrolets and Volkswagens
and Renaults pulled out of driveways?
Because they trained so hard
to climb the pinnacles,
and when they arrived the air
was thinner than they'd imagined,
the views predictable? Or because
they stood in gardens in the dark,
waiting for stars to fall
into their eyes, for new lovers
slimmer than the old,
with voices like the Adriatic
in calm weather? Is it because
they saw it at the ends
of black-and-white movies, too grainy
to be believed, but they believed,
and remembered Technicolor?
I tell you, we were among them.

So when we found it unexpectedly,
like the bed of four-leafed clover
under the dogwood,
we pronounced its name
with caution. We knew
the history of love,
had seen affection peel
like wallpaper
from our favorite rooms,
the motley patterns behind.

We are so pleased with ourselves,
each other, that we hug the luck
of our bodies every morning,

every night, our prayers
the same each time—
sweet words they'd shake
their heads at, sadly,
muttering, as we would
have muttered once,
of fools who think that life's
a valentine.

GRACE

Walking behind two men, I watch
the long tail of a pheasant drift
and rise, hanging half out
of a pocket made for it, feathers
caught in the small breeze
parting, coming together
like living things. They're September
colors, could make the quills
our neighbor says he'd write with
if he wrote.

The one with the bird has his shotgun
broken, its **V** slung over his shoulder
an echo of geese. The other
carries his gun in his arms, is calling
the spaniel, who chases a moth
into a ditch.

Dawn again. Sun's a pink slit
between mountains. I wait
for the crack of a shot to slice
the lightening sky. But all the birds
have disappeared—even the swallows
whose spiral above the balcony
at this hour is a mournful concert,
a skittery dance.

Pines in the distance begin to brighten,
deep blue to something like green.

Everything winged must be dreaming.

OCTOBER IN THE AUDE

It comes quickly to the mountains,
changeable winds that carry so many hawks
swooping, circling the same field,
Scott says it's a convention. The same day
we watch a parachute lesson,
a dozen men and women lifting turquoise,
red, fuchsia, brilliant yellow canopies
over their heads as they sprint downhill,
trying to catch a gust, like children
who hope an umbrella will hold them up,
take them over the trees. These silks
are colors you see only in dreams
of impossible flowers,
and they do rise for moments at a time.
The students' feet dangle, awkward,
then try to meet the ground—suddenly there
as it's always there. Even such brief
joinings with air, with absence,
must give them a sense that the world
can be left behind, that one can choose
the landscape of the mind. I imagine
their goal, small brushes with death
made beautiful, the spirit drifting off
where it will.

We take a picnic to the woods above them,
noticing, as we climb, the hawks'
continuing patterns, with and against
the wind. They are a kind of silent music,
notes on the blue, a rhythm that repeats,
slow loops I'd say were nocturnes
if this were night, and the long glissandos
of dives.

We find a spot in the trees where flakes
of light filter through, and then a whole
patch of it, bright, where the wind

doesn't enter. I think of snow, how Wisconsin
this time of year can already be glazed
with a white that mutes sound and difference.
Higher, where the Pyrenees define Andorre,
that may have begun. But here
in the foothills, we shed our jeans,
make love on the old blue bedspread
we keep in the car. Sun spills
into my eyes, a blinding that makes pines
disappear in a golden blaze, and we too
float on the quick heat that could be
midsummer. When shadows begin to darken
the grass, our skin wants clothes again.
We drive to the highest ridge,
where we can see a line of overlapping peaks
stretch hazily to Spain. We leave
before they disappear with the day.
Halfway back, the hawks still circle
toward dusk, a falling melody, the year
easing down.

THE PAL LUNCH

After Edward Hopper's *Nighthawks*, 1942

The year of my birth, my father's café.
But it's not my father behind the counter
bending to look for matches, a lock
of blond hair falling over his forehead
like a thought he brushes away. He stuffs
that hair back under the creased
white hat shaped like the soldiers' caps
they must all have worn, those short-order cooks
who were also the waiters, the owners.
He's commenting on the empty stools,
how he likes this hour, when people
are few, when most have drifted away,
their hands in their pockets.

No, my father's the one in the gray fedora,
my mother's beside him. In a reversal
like dream, they're the customers, leaning
easily on elbows, heavy white coffee mugs
steaming before them. He's just asked
for a light. He'd tried to strike up
a conversation with the man whose back
is to us, but no dice. That man is tired,
a little drunk. So the one behind the counter
and my father talk of the war, the draft.
They can't know the blond man will die in France
or that my father survives the Pacific.
My mother nods, her hands still slim,
white and delicate-veined as the peonies
she grows. This is long before arthritis
takes root in her fingers.
Huge coffee machines gleam silver
beside them, under fluorescent bulbs,
one buzzing off and on like a faint alarm.

They are not lonely, there in the bright café,
while darkness inhabits the street outside
where no cars are, neither parked nor moving.

They relax, for once the ones who sit, leisure
resting lightly on their shoulders.
They can go home and to bed whenever
they wish, to the house on Reuter Avenue,
the bedroom of soft chenille
and the oval mirror low enough
for a child, later, to see
her whole self in their image.
They will not have to rise before dawn
to come here, to heat the polished grill
and mix the pancake batter.

My father lights his fifth cigarette
in an hour. The smoke obscures their faces,
a cloud that passes over them quick as years.
My mother goes to the restroom,
puts on fresh lipstick, rearranges her hair.

My grandmother waits at home with me,
checking her watch, wondering
what could possess them,
where in the world they might be.

THE DIFFICULT LIFE OF IDEAS

They limp toward the horizon, hardly hearing
the birds cawing, calling—voices that skip
toward noon. They are concentrating,
they want to perfect themselves. There is longing
in their silence, their awkwardness,
but they cannot bring breath into themselves
by will. Rabbits skitter across the hills,
escaping guns. Chestnuts fall.
Farmers rumble by on tractors.
There's real pain in the walk uphill,
the sun's grown stronger. They stop to rest,
spirits diminishing in the heat. Now they wish
only for arrival, a house where they can lie down,
someone to feed them quail and plums.

POEM TO THE IDEAL READER

You are the twin my mother
gave away at birth,
suddenly arrived from out west,
Arizona, where you grew up
with horses and novels and Prokofiev,
your foster parents musicians.
While I thought you'd died,
you were listening to violin concertos
and training colts, waiting
for the day I'd flee the snow
and head for a land
of perpetual blossoms. (Even now,
as winter deepens, red and white camellias
bloom out the bedroom window.)
While you studied desert owls
and words, I ranged innocent
and lonely through the world—
to Spain and France and Italy,
to the sad Balkans. Now you are here,
your old Volkswagen piled to its ceiling,
the whole backseat, with books.
I take you for walks on the beach,
where we stop to watch porpoises—
new to us both—our hair tangling
in the wind. Whatever
lines I suggest, you nod,
your face telling me gently
yes or no. I sleep
so much better, you
in the next room, up reading
all night with candles.

WATCHING MYSELF COMPOSE

Only Peterson's shoe store had one—
a mahogany box you could stand against,
feet thrust into a space
where the x-ray promised and gave
a webbed vision,
thin bones gleaming green,
iridescent through the viewer.

I stretched my young spine to reach it,
to bend to the window,
the mystery revealed
like something forbidden,
its eerie image taking me back
somewhere before my own birth.

It was like seeing into the heart
of your life, when you
can nearly remember
the first steps you took,
how one trembling foot
went ahead of the other
and you were free, or could see
freedom coming, your own
legs taking you far, oh far
from home.

Whenever we passed that store,
I ran in to look: there was a way
to see growth, to see how to fit
outside to inside,
how to watch the self
compose over years

while the rays must have drifted
out through the room
where farmers sat
with their scraped-off boots
beside them, and young women

waited, their curls sleeked down
into hairpinned rolls
framing earnest faces,
some with babies beginning
inside them, each of them
smiling, each waiting
his turn, her turn.

WHAT IF

when you entered your mind
with purpose, you found not the field
you'd told yourself to imagine, the wild
strawberries of childhood strewn
among the tall grass where you lay
under apple trees, but a land flatter
and wider than sight could take in.
What if you forgot how to bring inside
the music that used to begin
in your gradual wakings, and in the space
before sleep, when rain began softly,
and all your sweet longings loosened.
What if traffic and telephones
continued their commerce, so loud
you couldn't remember how your skin felt,
floating. There is this fear
stalking the hours. One day
it might disappear, that place
you could go at will, where your own
voice hummed like a mother,
a crooning that let your blood
slow, the poem of the body
riding blue murmuring crests, naming
its love, loving its life.

JASMINE

Phan Thi Kim Phuc, now 22, travels throughout the U.S. giving speeches, raising money for plastic surgery to repair her scars.

Think of how you saw her first:
naked, nine, screaming,
her napalmed arms lifted
like wings that would not
rise. No relief, no matter
how far, how fast she fled
or imagined flying. Burns
on her back, her chest,
drilled in, spread out,
so that she thought
she was dying,
would disappear in one
of the agonized rushes
that licked off her skin.
We remember her mouth,
a dark moon of grief.

Nights she dreams
of fire drifting down,
her body a flower
whose petals curl and grow black
before they're quite open.

She feels herself
buried alive, her skin
peeling off in sheets
so that before sleep comes
she's already bones.

But clouds overhead now are only
clouds. In storms
rain is cool, sweet
water, like rivers
she swims in.

"Forgiveness,"
she tells the press,
is her body's reason

to travel a country
where some men remember
children exploding
in the air
beneath them,
fragments of flesh
floating down
from the sky.

Beauty rises up and says
to the beast,
"The war is over,
the past is the past."

The beast has been prowling
a long time now. He can
hardly hear that voice,
a lute in his ear.

Can scarcely see
through the shaggy hair
covering his eyes
the lilies blooming
before him.
But the scent—the scent
of jasmine on the air
begins to reach him.

How to be the forgiven?
All the grace
is in her.

May our scars lighten
to white, as they do
over years. Let each one
be a blossom, pure
as original pain
transformed, yet itself,
so that we cannot forget
what was there.

A lovely young woman leans
into the camera, hair falling

over her carefully
camouflaged shoulders.
As palm leaves fan
behind, we strain
to imagine the air
become jasmine.

IT BEGINS WITH A PRESENTIMENT

The way, when I was ill,
exhaustion came over me so fast
I knew I had to find a bed,
then fell instantly to sleep.
This is not sleep but something
closer to trance,
the scratch of pen on paper
already part of the music
that's coming, not in tune—
that shifts, the way a dream
slides, you're going right
when you could have sworn
the old farmhouse was to the left,
where dust kicked up by a palomino
still floats down,
forming a wreath around
a young girl's head.
All you can do is follow, meandering through the black-eyed
Susan ditch, humming the theme
from a movie. You will discover a barn where kittens drop
from their mother when you pick her up,
wet notes so small you have to magnify
the sound to hear it, to keep hearing it
for years. Where are you going?
You didn't know then,
though paradise was palpable
and lines of cedar
sheltered the path out.
Now you have a better idea
where it will end. But the going
remains fragrant, the blood
unaware of age, wild in its autumn heart
even as it notices, then counts
irregular beats.

CONTAINING THE LIGHT

> Yet I wonder if an image of the imagination is ever close
> to reality.
> —Gaston Bachelard

Disappearance is the fear—
not of the self, which can drone on
like November wind in Wisconsin,
on into December, through March,
even April, the ceaseless wind that sings
ghost songs through windows as tight
as a grandfather's carpenter hands
could make them. Between green swirls
of plaster and oak frames,
it varies its dissonant pitch,
but not the lament. No,
it's the past leaking out that keeps us
awake all night, keeps us making corrections.

Today the leaves are falling faster
than I can sweep them
from the patio. The sun is almost warm
on my back, the garden's colors deepen,
and old Octobers offer themselves.
What can be resurrected?
The way the light did not shatter
but bent our shadows against
sixth-century walls in Dubrovnik,
against cool stone, against
the promises of centuries, soon again
to be broken? Or how, the year
we married, the soft air of the village
was much like here in Carolina.
What blurs is how love takes
the fading light and turns it gold,
keeps turning it, in and out of itself,
while what burns burns deeper.

I think of a lonely road where pears
ripen, never quite sweetly,
and how it becomes the path
to a hill where a castle fallen to ruin

is partially rebuilt, then left
to itself again, blackberries thickening
the way back down to where the Virgin
reveals herself white as bone
as the trees begin to lose their amplitude.
Where do they rest, the falls
that gave us ourselves and led us here?
Their shapes grow skeletal,
the light paler, even as beauty
thins, pared to essentials.

LASTING

When the first radio wave music escaped Earth's
ionosphere, it literally did become eternal. Music, in
this century, has been converted from sound into the
clarity of pure light. Radio has superseded the
constraints of space.
                    —Leonard Shlain, *Art & Physics*

Imagine Vivaldi suddenly falling
on the ears of a woman
somewhere beyond Alpha Centauri,
her planet spun into luminescence
aeons from now. She might be
much like us, meditating
on the body, her lover murmuring
to the underside of her breast
before its heaviness suspends,
for a moment, the lift and pause
of his breath. A music she almost knows
drifts through centuries, startling,
augmenting her pleasure.
When earth is particles of dust,
Orson Welles may still strike fear
into the hearts of millions
who wake one morning, unaware
that light has arrived
as an audible prank. Ezra Pound might rasp
his particular madness from an Italy
still alive in arias that shower
into the open windows
of a world youthful as hope.
When books are no longer even ashes,
and no heart beats in any space
near where we were, suns
may intersect, and some of our voices
blend into choirs, the music of the spheres
adrift among new stars.

FROM *To Find the Gold* (1990)

THE GOLD SHE FINDS

On the Life of Camille Claudel, Sculptor

Sculpture is born of the need to touch, from the almost maternal joy of holding clay between one's hands.
> —Camille Claudel

I showed her where to find the gold, but the gold she finds is truly hers.
> —Auguste Rodin

Mlle. Claudel's sculpture is very different from Rodin's. She picks and gathers the light like a bouquet, unlike Rodin, who presents a compact block that shoves it back.
> —Philippe Berthelot

Camille Claudel is the most considerable woman artist at the present hour.
> —Camille Mauclair, 1895

Along with Berthe Morisot, Camille Claudel is the authentic representative of the female genius.
> —Gustave Kahn, 1905

In Paris, Camille mad . . . huge and looking filthy, speaking incessantly in a monotonous and metallic voice . . . one had to intervene . . . and there it is for thirty years.
> —Paul Claudel, 1909, 1911

1   The Little Chatelaine, *1870*

A pitcher shatters, red wine spilled
to the tiled kitchen floor
and spreading. It's a map, the child
thinks absently, tucking her feet
behind the chair rung. The usual
voices raised to the usual pitch
fly past her, a swarm of blackbirds.
Camille feels her mother's rage,
but it is like wind that can only leak in
around windows and doors, through
small cracks. Nothing to fear
when her face contracts,
or from her father's bellowing.
The child gives a sign
to her brother, excuses herself

and slips away. Animals rearrange
their bodies in the evening clouds,
where the faces of saints
are known to appear.
She spends half an hour, hoping
for Our Lady of Fatima,
who keeps herself busy, embroidering.
By bedtime, the moon is a cousin
who died last year. His face tells Camille
he suffered—the pockmarks still there,
his brow crinkled. André, she calls
through the trees, and hearing
no answer, answers her mother.

2   *Sister and Brother in the Forest of*
    Villeneuve, 1879

They climb to the few flat stretches
of massive stone that jut, savage monuments,
to the sky. Clothes thrown aside,
they sit, she clutching her knees,
he leaning back on an elbow, a book open
next to him. He reads to her—
Alfred de Vigny. His own poems show a mass
of chestnut hair to her hips, and blue eyes
he describes as a color encountered
only in novels. As Paul's light skin
grows pink in the sun, she sketches him,
page after page of young Roman,
that sweet torso lithe as birch.

Thunderclouds move in with the stealth
of their mother. When the rain comes,
lashing them in a sudden wind, they struggle
into wet clothes gleefully, slide down,
then dash to their small cave, with its cache
of candles. In hazy light, her joke drawings,
made to look prehistoric, take on
a luminous glow. A small horse
leaps across one wall, a dart in its flank.

3   *The Meeting, 1884*

My dear Paul,

Today I met the master, Rodin!
Do you remember my meeting
at the École des Beaux-Arts?
How after M. Dubois saw my bust
of you, the one when you're
thirteen, he asked if I were
Rodin's student? That Rodin.
When he took me into his studio
where he's in the midst of an epic,
The Gates of Hell—incredible work!—
I trembled. Paul, some of the figures
looked like mine—especially
the women's features, but there's a weight,
an authority, that's not me.
And M. Rodin himself—well. He's got eyes
like diamonds, that look as if he's trying
to drill to the bottom of everyone,
and a great shaggy head, with a nose
imperious as yours, but bigger!
When he talks his nostrils flare.
He has the air of a nervous horse, always
in motion, starting at noises,
and skinny legs that almost prance.
He took one long look at *Old Helen*
and my *Bust of a Woman with Closed Eyes*,
and announced that I'd be his assistant.
This alone, little Paul, was worth
the move to Paris. I'll be helper,
student, apprentice, and do my own work.
It's as if I'd lived the rest of my life
in the forest, not knowing that all paths out
would join in one distant spot—right here.

4   *Note to Rodin after* Sea Foam, *1884*

Nothing prepared me for this.
Not even those first giddy weeks

when we talked of taking a steamer
to Africa, leaving everyone behind.
Before I met you I thought I knew
the human form, but what I know now
is deeper than skin and muscle,
deeper than bone. You discovered
something quiet in me, and made it grow,
just as you lift a breast in your hands,
gently blowing, breathing
more life into it. I am no longer
that country girl with talent,
but a woman whose joy has found
its voice in marble.

5   The Eternal Idol, *1887*

My dear Paul,

Imagine my surprise this morning,
walking into the studio to find
M. Rodin sitting before two models
posed like lovers, the woman
on her knees on a low table,
leaning back and holding her toes
with her hands, perfectly balanced,
the man kneeling before her, pressed
into her, his head between her breasts,
his mouth more caress than kiss on her
white skin. All the while,
M. Rodin was sketching, frenzied,
throwing one piece of paper
after the next to the floor. My *Cacountala*,
in clay, stood in the corner, like
a mirror to these lovers, who, if they
shifted position slightly, could see
themselves in elemental form. It was
as if my figures had been touched by a god
and brought to life. Everything was silent
except for the sound of ripped paper
and Rodin's breathing—always louder
than anyone's! The models, though,

for the first five minutes I stood there,
didn't seem to breathe at all.
It was like a dream

broken by a bird hitting the window.
The couple unfolded themselves, and Rodin
and I went for a coffee. Paul, he had
tears in his eyes, and told me—oh
many things. Rose, he says,
is getting arthritic, her knees creak
when she walks, and sometimes it's painful
even to get up out of her chair.
Poor Rose. It would be awful to be old.
But worse for him, who feels he lives
inside his own Gates of Hell (no wonder
that work has all the pathos of his genius!)—
his son always sick,
and that woman. Paul, I feel his spirit
in me, and when my hands are filled with clay,
I have the texture of flesh in my fingers
long before the casting, I know the tension
in each tendon, the way eyes hold
their memories intact, how sorrow
animates a body, even in rapture.

6   *The Tower of the Château d'Islette
    in Touraine, 1887*

In this vast cylinder
we are dancers floating
up a spiral staircase
to the room where dozens
of arrow slits let in
the moon's damp light,
making a crown of leaves
across your forehead.
I love my whole body
wet, exhausted.
Each foggy dawn
I lie in half sleep.
Always those fingers open

my thighs, your big hands
warm as the rising sun,
while swallows circle outside.
At noon we stand on the bridge,
tossing chunks of bread
to the lazy trout.
I like to complain
of my muscles aching.
You grin.
You put a piece of brioche
on my tongue and say,
Here is my flesh.
All afternoon and evening
wind churns the light until,
red as burgundy, it follows
us back to bed.

7 "Le Clos Payen," 1888

Her art has the inner light, is perforated, cut out like stained glass, it welcomes and captures the light. It is in this way that her art resembles the art of jade.
    —Philippe Berthelot

My dear Paul,

The house M. Rodin rented for us
is falling to ruins, but it has charms.
I've been sweeping
cobwebs from the salon we'll use
for work, which at first looked
like our old cave—the light
through those dirty windows so dim
we found a bat contentedly sleeping,
dangling from the chandelier.
Paul, he had the bedroom
redone as a surprise for me—but frankly,
just between us, it has the look
of a bordello, great heavy drapes
of velvet (red!) trimmed in gold.
There's a Louis XIV dressing table

I do like, and a scrolled
hand mirror with distorted glass
that makes me look a bit fat,
though it's gorgeous. I think he found it
at the flea market. Most important,
we can get away from Rose,
who's begun to hound him.

I make him cassoulet and roasted lamb,
even attempted a tarte the other day—
peach—that wasn't bad.
I plan work on a figure I'll call
Young Woman with a Sheaf. I have
the drawings already, know everything
about her stance, a certain modesty
she'll suggest, but I haven't yet
got the expression. I've also just made
a drawing of you, my dear, in colored
pencil. It's your pouty look,
the one that enchants the girls.
I hardly need you to pose any more,
your face is so clear
it rises to greet me mornings.
Lately I don't remember my dreams,
though some days I wake with a sense
of colors swirling around me, great
sweeps of it. Maybe that girl
with the sheaf has made a broom,
is replacing the debris of this house
with deep blues and purples, like sky
just before sunrise.

8   *Letter to Rodin from the Château
     d'Islette in Touraine, Where
     Camille Went Alone, Perhaps
     Pregnant, 1889*

Seigneur,

I'm writing you again because
I have nothing else to do. And to tell you

it's wonderful here—the hay's just
been cut, and the wheat and oats,
and the meadow smells of lavender.
Madame C. tells me that if we like
we can take all our meals
in the small conservatory that looks
both ways to the garden.
I had lunch there today, and it's
lovely—every color imaginable
of that flower I'd rather not name,
and dahlias, giant and dwarf,
and hollyhocks and yellow lilies.
She tells me I can bathe in the river.
Her daughter and the maid do,
and it's perfectly safe.
Would you mind? It would save me
trips to the baths in Azay
and I could use that time to sketch.

Love, I sleep naked to let myself pretend
you're here, but the mornings
are so disappointing. Please hurry!
Would you buy me a dark blue
bathing suit, please—if you can
find it—with white piping. Try
the Bon Marché.

Above all, no more deception.
Keep your promise and we'll be
in paradise.

9 "La Demoiselle Élue," 1890

*Ah! I really loved her and with all the more sad ardor by the evident
signs I felt that never would she take certain steps to engage her whole
spirit and that she was keeping herself inviolable against queries to her
heart's solidity.*
        —Claude Debussy, in a letter to Robert Godet

My dear Paul,

Do you recall the musician I mentioned
I'd met at Robert Godet's? Debussy?

I care nothing for music normally,
as you know, but how I wish you could hear
him play. It takes me back to Villeneuve.
I can see us whirling across those fields
from the giant rocks, a pair of hummingbirds,
and he gives me the feeling too
of poems you read me that summer
you were twelve, and I was sixteen.
Something about him lets me be a girl
again, Paul. A splendid man!
I fear refusing him
is another grand mistake. Rodin
is jealous. Fine. He has his tarts.
In truth, I'm close to Claude the way
I'm close to you—and he's a refuge
from that world where the pain keeps spreading.
I begin to think our saggy-skinned Rose
is installed forever, no matter
that she shakes her fist at him every day.
Most of the time, I feel my own youth
draining away like an August stream.
Affection ebbs too, yet I can't
make a break. I try to fall in love
with Claude, who's my age, and adores me.
He's adopted my passion for Japanese drawing
and says he'd give up green-eyed Gabrielle.
So why does that pot-bellied old man
keep my soul? He's like a cancer
that creates a gorgeous fever,
all the while gnawing away at the heart
of everything.

10   *Letter to Rodin from Touraine, 1893*

What joy to wake from a dream of you
and not desire you! All this time,
my hands busy in plaster, you occupied
my body like a tenant. Wherever
I turned I saw women with your eye,
their flesh blushing under my frank look.

Mornings the windows filled with pollen,
and I laughed, feeling your beautiful
sneeze—the way you throw your whole
head back, like a fine horse neighing.
Today I wonder if you're rowing
on a lake somewhere with a girl
whose auburn hair makes her partly
me. I don't even care. I'm separate
just now, I'm Camille, who drinks
beer alone in a café, the buzz of voices
around her like a waltz,
wanting only earth between her fingers,
earth under her feet.

11   *Notes for* The Vanished God; *or,*
The Beseecher, *1894*

*At last you were "yourself," totally free of Rodin's influence, your
imagination was as great as your craft.*
        —*Letter from Eugene Blot to Camille Claudel, 1932*

I want to feel the weight of her knees
on the stone, and the pain
of kneeling there so long, but she
will have gone beyond the physical,
into a realm where he is all
that can touch her. Eyes and arms will lift
in an agony of prayer,
she'll be pure supplication,
and may be pregnant.
There'll be a sense that she knows
the outcome, does not expect
the god to relent or reappear.
But there is nothing else for her.
She'll ache for him without faith,
without choice, in sheer despair.

12 Three Works, 1895–1897

i *Maturity*, plaster, 1895

My dear Paul,

I fear it's more and more hopeless.
It's as if he's a tree grown
with branches intertwined
in another, one gnarled and stronger
with age, and he can't disentangle
himself without snapping
too many limbs. Never mind
that my green shoots got mingled
with his.

At last, I've got us in plaster.
Mother Rose with her fist clenched
against me, he with his arm
clasped around her, protecting her.
I'm on my knees as always,
clutching his hand, and he's turned
to her even as his body yearns
in my direction. In bronze,
it will be more mythic, but
for now, we're ourselves, raw.
The harpy wins.

ii *The Little Chatelaine II*, 1895

My dear Paul,

I keep trying to get *The Little Chatelaine*
right, less haunted, but the eyes
stay blind, the face more grieved
than mine in every conception.
Some days I'm not sure which of us
came first. My hair too was braided like that
at seven. I can still feel Mother
yanking it, making me cry, and telling
you and Louise that I was a baby.
You and lovely Louise, who did

all the right things—married, produced
proper children. Paul, tell me the truth
when you come next month. Look
into my eyes and see if you see the shadow.
Look at her and tell me who I am.

iii   *Clotho*, Marble, 1897

After all, the body knows just as much as the soul, the details of the
anatomy are worth those of psychoanalysis.
      —Paul Claudel

Toothless, breasts
crumpled paper, she can scarcely
carry the dross of her life,
hair a mass of twisted ropes
that weigh on her head,
so that she must tilt it
to one side, even to stand.

How many times have a man's hands
gripped the old woman's calves?
Pressing loose skin,
does he bruise her ankles?

She sees her path,
even with rheumy eyes,
and keeps her direction.

13   *Note to Rodin from Rue de Turenne,*
     1898

I've taken a new studio, in the Marais.
Never mind where, exactly.
This is just to tell you where I won't be.
Don't look for me. I want no
letters, no word from you at all,
unless it's to tell me Rose is dead,
and you poisoned her! Or that you're publishing
a confession, listing all your crimes
against me. Too late for anything else.
Everything you've said has turned to salt,

it penetrates the cracks in my skin,
so that I work all day with a sense
that my whole body's burning.
There's nothing more to say.

14   *Quai Bourbon, 1900*

My dear Paul,

This morning I woke with the taste of him
on my tongue. I spit and spit,
and the cats thought I was funny.
Too much work to do to think of him.
And the door is bolted. After my neighbor,
M. Picard, broke in with a passkey
and took back sketches of my *Yellow Woman*,
I learned to be careful.
Yellow women have appeared in two salons—
with Rodin's signature, of course!
Oh, he rakes it in—millions of francs
on my ideas. I wonder who's doing
his feet, who's carving eyes,
who poses for goodbyes and betrayals.
Rose was his model once, you know.
I saw her the time the cleaning woman
put drugs in my coffee, and I was out
for twelve whole hours. She was young,
swirling in bronze, then gold,
suspended from the ceiling—
then standing still, in stone.
Did you know she comes to my window
at night, peers in at me, sleeping?
I can hear her breath on the glass,
then a sound of choking.

15 Dust, 1907

Your bust is no more. It lived the life of roses.
        —Camille Claudel, in a letter to Henry Asselin

My dear Paul,

July again, and nothing survives.
I begin to like my ritual:
all year I work as if the salons
were knocking on my door each week,
as if M. Dupin were waiting
for his commissions. I go out
into the streets to draw the people—
I want, now, my statues so distinct
from robber Rodin's that never
will anyone ask questions.
I choose a woman sweeping her doorstep,
her hair brushed back from her forehead,
not quite carelessly; a fat butcher
in his shop, a cleaver raised
in his hand; men building a fountain
in the square. Last week I saw two
on a scaffold, their brown arms lifting
sparkling pink granite. One's body was bent
powerfully in two by the weight,
and I'd already got them both in clay.
They're gone too. Everything.
I take the hammer and smash
whatever's there—clay, plaster,
marble, stone. It flies into the air
and becomes a million brilliant stars.
For hours, as the dark comes in, they go on
shining. I like to wander
through the debris, before the carter
comes to bury it. Now is the third
anniversary of my new life.

My dear Charles,

It's true—they locked me up! The very day
your letter came to tell me about Papa's death.
They buried him and didn't say

a word to me. Just as in Paris, the breath
of Rodin has soured the air at Villeneuve.
He meets the family secretly. They're tethered

to him the way I was, especially that naive
Louise, my sister, who won't confess
to anything. A hundred thousand francs he bleeds

the public for, while the cats and I eat less
all the time, with no commissions to feed us.
When those brutes came to take me away—Blessed

Mary!—I begged them to let me smash
a few last things. Old casts of *Perseus*, four
fine ones, stood against one wall. They laughed.

I tried to write you then, but a nurse tore
up my letters. Mother wants to ban
me from writing anyone, calls me a whore

and lets me freeze here at Montdevergues, land
of the dying crazies. They scream day and night.
And the food! Worst in first class—it comes from cans

dribbled with poison. That's why I'm right
to stay in third, though I cook for myself
in any case—potatoes and eggs. It frightens

me how grateful I am to fill my poor shelf
once in a while with things from home—coffee,
sugar, soap, brandied cherries, half-melted

butter. Mother is kind about food, awfully
concerned for my health. But she never comes, never
answers my questions. Everyone says I'm softer

now, even docile. I'm sure I'd get better
at Villeneuve. I'd keep to myself—no sculpture—
nothing to make Mother angry. I could sit forever

in that garden, even forget the machinations of the monster
and his hag. I want the valley, those dark hills, my brother.

17   *Dreams, 1920*

My dear Paul,

This morning I woke to the sound
of a human voice in the chimney.
I knew who it was, for the night
had been filled with him. Months now,
I've had separate lives, the nightmare
day with its shrieking faces in every corner,
its greasy inedible soup, and the long
hours of my own silence, when the clouds
that used to hover over Villeneuve
descend around my head, so I
can scarcely see beyond the length
of my arm. Then the monster assumes
his proper form, and I'm on my guard.
But the nights! I'm taken back years,
to a bed in Touraine, to the bed
in La Folie Neubourg, to the studio
on Rue de l'Université. He takes me
in his arms. I'm twenty, nearly fainting
with desire. He's a volcano—unstoppable—
and I love his power, those enormous
insistent hands. Beautiful lies!

Sometimes I sculpt *Sea Foam* again—
that glistening marble torso
me, stretched on a tongue of onyx.
I strike a pose, he strides in,
strokes my hair and the curve of my back,
and I peer into his eyes.
I find them innocent! You must
be right. My mind turns itself
upside down.

Last things shall be
first, first last, love and hate
will clasp hands, whirl in a circle,
let go, and fall to the ground.

18 *From the Asylum at Montdevergues,
    1938*

My dear Paul,

I wait for the visit you promised me
next summer, but I don't hope for it.
Paris is so far away, and God knows
what may happen.

At this holiday time I always dream
about Mother. I never saw her again
after the day you sent me to asylums.
I'm thinking of the portrait I did
of her in our garden—those large eyes
with their secret sadness, resignation
over her whole face, hands crossed
on her knees in total abnegation.
I never saw the portrait again either.
Surely that odious creature
I try not to name wouldn't have stolen
that too? Not a portrait of my mother!

From time to time they pretend
to improve my lot here, but it doesn't last.
It's a sham. Lately they built
a big kitchen, one kilometer away.
That gave me an outing and a walk.
Now I'm ordered not to go there anymore—
no reason. Oh how I long
to be in a real house, to be able
to shut the door properly.

My dear Paul, you poor, sweet man—
they set you up in their game
without your even noticing.
The doctors said I could go home

years ago. Mother wouldn't have me
at Villeneuve. But you? You tell me
God has mercy on the afflicted,
God is good, etc. Let's talk about God,
who lets an innocent woman rot.

19   *Manna, September, 1943*

So much I finally understand—
how the spirit is nourished
by raisins and milk, how the days
disappear when you stay in bed,
so that one kind face bent
over your own is much
like another. Cakes arrive
in the mail from Paul.
I say to God, my cup
runneth over. I know
what it means. They tell me
I'm thin as a pine, but I eat
those gifts of jelly and butter,
I let sugar cubes melt on my tongue.
I remember pleasure,
my hands wet in plaster. I watch
a parade pass by my window, a line
of statues in bronze and marble,
bodies contorted, rising
and smiling, their lives
nearly over. Now they're erect,
growing younger
and younger, everything backward,
everything white.

NOW IS THE SILENCE OF SLEEPING DOVES

Of the neighbor's cough
quieted by codeine.
The silence of lovers
who've already forgotten
how the moon came to whiten
their open bodies. Now the hour
when breath wakens the skin
with its pauses.
From out of that stillness
a dog barks, then howls
as if the whole night
had been waiting,
as if, the dark being cleft
by that sound, all the wedges
could fall, deeper and deeper.

GENÊT

For Daryl

This is for you, who loved him, though
you never met, except through words
like high notes making a long glissando
down the page.

I've just learned that my favorite
French wildflowers, ones
with long bright stems and heavy clusters
of yellow blossoms, bear his name.
Yesterday I gathered them in heaps, the way
I did last summer, remembering
how one big brandy snifter lets them
fill half a room.

You'll like it that they have to be cut
with a knife, they're that tough,
and that it's hard to wedge the stems
between rocks set in the glass base
to keep them from tipping over.

A year ago I walked through these same fields
and didn't know the names of anything.
Margueritas filled my smaller vases,
and I called them daisies.

My friend Edmund spends his time
writing Genêt's biography. Another
act of love this chilly summer,
when no one knows how long
the season can last.

All year I have been redefining love.
You know about that. I wish you could know
the fragrance that fills this house.
I wish I could give you time
in these mountains, and brilliant genêts.

AFTER THIRTY OCTOBERS

This weather brings back Sunday
after church, reading the St. Paul paper,
the fragrance of lemon pie drifting
into the living room. Gary's stretched
on the floor with the funnies. David's pulling
boxing gloves off and on, caressing
his own soft fists. Mary Jo brings me
grape juice in a glass so small I tease her—
it's Second Communion. Not yet a beauty,
her almond eyes are magnified
behind thick glasses. She's seven and I'm fifteen,
drowsy against the heat register we dispute over.
Dad's alive, coming in from the meadow
where he's been talking with horses. This afternoon
he'll make fence—the sorrel, Flame, following,
nuzzling his back. Dinner's ready,
Mother's heaping pork chops onto a platter.
The grapefruit tree in the corner has spread
its leaves to the steam wafting out from the kitchen,
is fuller and greener than it will be
again. When the phone rings it's the boy
I'll marry, who's on his way, innocent
as the Siamese cat who suddenly drags
used Kotex all over the house. I run room
to room, scooping up bloody pads. Sun streams
into the cage of the new canary, who's just
stopped singing. Through the window we watch
tall field grass ripple and change, bend deep
and white in wind. I go out to stand in it,
as under the darkening sky, it's become ocean.

NEW PHYSICS

And if we should collide with such force,
might we fly off in different directions
and disappear, leaving, in our place,
some new combination that isn't us, really?
I've always imagined your fear
was something like that, even before
there was a language to explain it. Now
I think I partly understand
your flight, after love, from the room
where we watched through open windows
the stars and their discrete pulsing.

I speak of this, of you, as if we were
still present tense, as if you hadn't
once more approached the rim of my life,
that wobbly circumference, then chosen,
again, a safe trajectory. Once a month,
on schedule, I retrace those paths
as if there were something new I could learn,
some variable I might change,
and the world would be different.

Even these thousands of miles
do not annihilate your pull.
When you are asleep and dreaming,
I turn toward the visible moon, pale
in a daytime sky, and feel myself spinning.

PARIS AUBADE

Breathing, the last possession
that counts, comes faster here, where
time and our oldest obsessions

make us more conscious—self-conscious. The air
is completely polluted, of course, but haze
that descends on this city is like the fair

skin of Doris Day, filmed in the days
when soft light meant dropping gauze
in front of the camera. It's like that these lazy

first weeks when we stay in bed until noon, lawless
as coupling cats we hear on the balcony, late.
We inhale each morning as if the flawed

fabric of earlier lives had been laid
in a drawer, carefully folded, forever.
Yet under the net of that dream, we pay

for what we know. Bodies that flail under covers
all hours in pleasure learn to count breaths—
just after. Though the world falls away for lovers

as they make the escape into flesh,
its heavy atmosphere fills them. Clouds
are the color of nipples. Worn silk thins to mesh.

LAURA

And now we are three—one of us
still swathed in the scarves
of childhood, peeling them off, one
after another, pastel cotton plaids
giving way to silk in a range
of tulip colors. She emerges
with her dark hair tangled,
the way she likes it.

And what if this is not just
the beginning, what if this is
the moment we pass without noticing,
when the senses tell us everything
we'll know? She can sniff a star-white
flower on the side of the road
and say when it released its pollen,
when its embroidered blossoms
will become dust.

She consumes the planets with her
perfect vision, with a red telescope
set on the balcony table. All night
we hear her above us, shifting
position, taking notes on the universe.

AU PREMIER COUP

There are moments we record
so indelibly that when
the smell of popcorn, say, or
a phrase from Grieg wafts across
the room, you see a mother
standing at a Bathinette,
a baby fat and slippery under her hands,
piles of cotton diapers on a shelf
in three neat stacks, white
as blossoms. It's a quarter
of a century ago, and more.
You're young as the cherry tree
outside the opalescent window.
In your dreams, you sit in its branches,
looking through the glass
at yourself, bathing the child.
Framed like that, you're held,
the picture's surface
opaque, no underpainting
showing through. Someone
shakes an aluminum pot
in the kitchen. The sounds
of popping corn are grace
notes falling through the evening air.

TO ENTER

On marble sculpture by Nicolae Fleissig

Believe that veined wings heavy as memory
might, any moment, fold from the spine
of sorrow and take off into night.
Now, under moonlight, they lean
toward a curve of back, rest against flesh.

Prepare for a book of water in wind, for pages
open to the sun, music on stands rippling
black under plane trees. Yes, here are the closed
petals of sex, there is a head
like the whole body of a jellyfish, translucent
inside its pale helmet.

Think of a man with wooden blinders, each
painted with ancient worlds, so that when
they are shut, he contemplates golden dragons,
bracelets with rubies circling
bone-white arms. When the panels are open,
the light coming in is pain.

Though teeth grin the body's defiance,
the body's knowledge, mountains are rising
from plains.

There are paths to lost cities, to the heart's
magnificent ruins.

FROM *The Beautiful Noon of No Shadow*
(1986)

IN THE ABSENCE OF ANGELS

We want to believe
in the ones who take their children
to the zoo in strollers, murmuring
at lions and giraffes, their faces
lined with patience and sun. We think
they have never known days
when they must identify morning
by the relative lightness of gray,
have never felt autumn
rest on their hearts like fever.
But many, even of these,
must climb long ladders toward dawn.

I remember a decade of dark
when sometimes I walked
as if in the nightmare of chase,
my steps slow, as through deep snow.
Now I see, in child, lover and friend,
the same cellophane look in the eyes,
the same absence of angels,
and I ask again, into afternoon light,
how can we learn to be who we are
in the beautiful noon of no shadow?

THE DREAM OF BIRDS

Again it was one I forgot
to feed. Sometimes
there are whole cages of finches,
cockatiels, parakeets
living, but barely,
on seed moldy with age,
and no water. This time
it was the peach-faced lovebird
I once let go from his cage
in a climate he might
have survived in. He flew
to sit on the fence and call back,
his shrill chirp bewildered,
angry. At last he went
into a pine and away—
those iridescent tail feathers,

turquoise and green,
I used to collect when they fell
and send in letters to friends—
gone. In the dream
early this morning, it was
that bird. My heart went
dark with remorse. I could feel
the blood filling it, fast,
the way love does, and that regret.

WHEN THERE IS NO SURFACE

When there is no surface to rise through,
when lake and sky lose their separation
as dream and waking sometimes do,

so that the dream dreams emancipation
from itself, and you can wake over and over
inside the dream—then a breathless suspicion

blooms and scatters its strange flowers
through the memory, which wants to know
what it loves, and who he is that towers

above sleep and sleeplessness and grows
even as his absence becomes greater.
Was he a stranger whose affections flowed

into rooms you hadn't guessed? Much later
you think so. But when he is so much
part of you, you cannot believe you were the creator

of this myth, that it was half illusion. Such
love breathed through us, it became the air,
you sigh, grief and conviction mixed, the clutch

at the heart when you cry it bearable
only because you cannot yet concede that perfection
was something else, and is gone. *Unfair,*

you whisper when his friends speak of his defection
and insist they can't imagine anyone so right for him
as you are. You try to see him as the mere projection

of your wishes. But you had those nights, and swim
even now in the streams of that desire,
unable to release the self's dark twin.

THE SUDDEN APPROACH
OF TREES

The glittery video flashes
and the scene repeats. Directly
in that line of vision,
I keep driving
fast down the highway,
two cars ahead of me
passing each other wildly
until the collision,
the road going on and on
through flat green fields
toward a bright horizon.

I know this highway.
Soon there'll be
a restaurant on the left,
a dark place, nearly hidden
in trees. Upstairs, a hotel
where a woman stands
in a corridor,
a man she loves in a room
on one side, his son
across the hall, playing
with cards he spreads on a blanket.
The child is curious, pleased
this stranger has come
to them. The father, nervous,
steps into the corridor once,
brings the woman an apple,
touches her hair.

They hear cars going by
on the highway,
the same sequence of cars,
over and over.
Two pass each other,
just there, before
the dark building.

Each time,
a third one follows,
seeming to slow
at the sudden approach
of these shady trees.

WHEN LOVE BECOMES

the too-bright flower
of your death opening, you stop,
the image arresting your hands.

I try to imagine those velvety petals, or silk—
the pink lining of coffins, rich invitations
to lie down and down.

Waiting for you to return to your body, and mine,
I suddenly see the diaries
shelved on the walls of your dreams.

Now years are being torn and tossed
out the night window,
and in the blue light

from the towel-draped lamp,
I stand at your side and watch pages
float to the ground.

THE ROOM

I stumble, nearly breaking
my heel, into a wide room
lighted from the floor.
Faces are shadowed like buildings,
their rich contours etched,
the folds like blinds
at the windows.
If we look into mirrors,
we'll see our grandparents.
I too am a stranger here.

Next to me
a woman is telling a story.
She has been living
her whole adult life
here on the 17th floor.
She has no husband, no children,
but labors each day
in film. Whatever
the director wants,
she does. No, she
is no actress,
but types, carries props,
urges recalcitrant stars
to come out on time.
She has seen herself
on screen, always played
by someone else.
She likes this room,
the way plants bend down
their leaves, as if they're
listening to the couple below.

A man appears
in the doorway
carrying leaves—
whole handfuls of leaves—

the way a child
brings them in
to the first-grade teacher.
He places them
(oak and maple; it's fall)
on a long glass table.
Through the light
coming up, they're paler
than I'd have imagined,
but brilliant too,
translucent, of course,
and waxy, as if
that same child
had treated them,
making them last
a long time.
When the man
puts his hands
palms down on the table
next to the leaves,
all the veins are similar.

I walk to the window
where cardinals gather
beneath a birch.

No, no birch here—
and we're too high
for streetlamps
to show any feathers,
even deep red.
It must be reflection
from the tall
woman's dress,
its scarlet pattern,
her long white arms.

I take a drink
from a tray
being passed
by a black-suited teenager.
I choose a pale one,

not sure
what each silver-rimmed glass
contains.

In the next room
someone has switched on
a television.
Through the door
the screen flashes,
though the sound
is too low to hear.

For awhile
I fall asleep
on the pillows
stacked in a corner—
a blue and a red one,
another, ten-colored
and huge. They block
the light coming up
so it's easy to dream.

I wake aware
that the party
is still going on.
Hardly anyone's moved.

It's late enough now
for the sun,
that beginning dawn
diluting the light
still beating
inside.
I hear my heart.

I look into the bowl
of lilies
that seem to be growing
though their stems
have been cut

and they're held
in their places by wire.
They nod next to the wine.

The light is still rising.

MIRACLES

Think of it, he says, and tells me
how water from a burst pipe
spewed straight out, so far
into the startled air
it didn't harm the cupboard under it,
shelves piled high with her drawings,
lithographs, diaries,
though it came cascading
down the stairs.
He could hear it
when he put his key in the door,
the sound like his heart exploding,
imagining all her images gone.

The family sent him snapshots,
the marker of her grave
and the sculpture—
marble arms embracing a torso—
the only two objects untouched
by a blizzard piling snow
everywhere else in New Hampshire.
He points to forsythia on the hill,
unrecognizable,
but her name
blazes from gray stone.

It was a death sudden
as today's surprising snow.
In a moment the sky darkened
and then the air was white.
When the sun came out
seconds later,
nobody could believe
there'd been such change.

In a large white room
one of her plaster figures

leans forward: a woman's body
inlaid with speckled feathers,
not so much poised for flight
as seeming to watch the floor
as if it might dissolve
at her feet,
becoming sky, snow, water
she could fall through,
lifting at last
her small gray wings.

POINT OF DISAPPEARANCE

A young man threatens to throw himself
in front of the metro. Weaving, waving
his drunken arms in apparent rage, he yells

at the nearby *clochard*, "I don't want to be saved!"
Meanwhile, onlookers line the quai
in cautious, curious silence. A man, braver

than the rest of us, pulls him back. The boy stays
out of danger long enough to let the train come in
but is pushing the good Samaritan away

when I get on. I watch him lurching, thin
with too-quick growth and all the wrong foods,
I imagine. And I think of that age trimmed

of its myths. At times in a foolish mood
I've said I'd give up all I've learned to be 18 or 19
in Paris, forgetting then how the blood flew

through me like the runaway train I'd seen
in a film, and how the crash was always
a moment away. How the sweet machine

of the body, in perfect ease, could go days
without sleep, but the spirit darkened
quick as a full eclipse before any maze

of choices. A word could sharpen
pain to nearly unbearable grief; a smile
that felt indifferent from one who happened

into my path of attraction was a trial
I might fail, and break down in public, weeping.
Death was an alternative to everyone else's mild

acceptance of the world's devouring
loneliness. Not a few of us considered it.
But now, I read, even more of the young are leaping

from bridges, lying on tracks, their gift
to themselves mere absence
of all that emotion. I see my son lift

his head to examine his awkward presence
in a hall of mirrors. He locates
on a shimmering surface his point of disappearance.

THE ORIGAMI HEART

Can the heart be folded like paper?
I saw it, the four corners
making four points
facing a center, the beginning
of something.
Hard to think of it flat and white,
though how it flattens and fades
is easy enough.

I am touched by the words of a man
I don't know. He heard
the woman he loves
on the phone to her other lover.
He still sees her face
as it was when he entered the room.
It stays there, like the moon
through the nearest window,
even on cloudy nights, so that when
he comes into the kitchen
he sees her again
even if she's in bed asleep.

My moon is a sliver I can't see.
It's rained all day.
But two nights ago it was crescent,
the shape of a folded wing.
Bodiless, it hovered above my dreams,
above my heart
imagining itself
a white bird sent sailing.

IN RILKE'S PARIS

Today I wake to his meditations
on the city. While he laments
the violin next door to every
room he takes, and the men playing,
who might otherwise walk
into rivers, I listen to my neighbor
pick up his flute and trill
the morning in like an island bird.
Often jobless, he must feel despair.
But what I hear through the wall
is the low laugh of a man
who turns his back on darkness,
a woman's rippling voice, lovemaking
punctuated by song (he sometimes
sings joyous scales in the middle—
no words), and always, always,
the poet's dream—
"the winged energy of delight."

TRAVELING IN THE OLD COUNTRY

For my mother

From Oslo we glide
through mountains gray as ash,
peaks piled with predictable snow,
and all the way down
awkward trees bent chilled
to the rain. There at the base,
an occasional red house
defies the landscape.
Mud pooled in swirls
has frozen into pattern.
"Lovely," you shudder, "but not
to live here."

As darkness settles,
the light inside grows brighter,
the outside contours
disappear into haze,
so that my photographs
(the fluorescent train light
gleaming at the margins)
will come back black and white.

Look at the woman beside us.
Her reflection in the smoky window
is yours ten years from now—
mine too.

In a restaurant in Bergen,
beams cracked with the weight
of the roof, the old joints
unsealed by age,
you stand at an empty table
set for a dozen guests,
crystal glittering
like stars we can see
this one clear night.

For an instant
you look nearly as old as you are,
and the place, out of an Ibsen play,
seems like home, though not any
home we ever knew.

This is how I often think of you—
familiar foreign town,
room pungent with fish
and strong coffee.
Not on cozy Reuter Avenue
with my secret room
behind the built-in drawers,
and the attic
with its overflowing trunks;
not in our ranch house on the hill
surrounded by horses;
not in the little bungalow
where you live now,
defining yourself
as unexpectedly
as you consented to come here.
Back home, "up there," as you call it,
new man, new friends,
long walks in the snow,
and dancing.

In the street market I look
for lutefisk.
"Not so," you've always claimed
when I say it's soaked in lye.
But the seller nods yes,
and I grin.

Our last Norwegian meal
you order in the hotel dining room
while I bring down the bags
and check us out.
"Marinated salmon," you say
when I join you.
It comes slippery and bright
as a page of finger paint,

raw, not what you intend.
We laugh as you drink coffee
in the airport, killing
the taste.

What can we say to each other
at these moments in our lives?
Sometimes we are simply
two women who compare
the notes of generations.
Today we buy the same blouse.

You leave, beautiful now as a girl,
returning to another North.
The world rocks
as we cross seas and oceans
toward and away from ourselves.

ELEGY

How can I say this—
that the first betrayal
was his,
that he stood me on a table
saying, Jump, I'll catch you,
and when I jumped
he did,
then chastised me:
Trust nobody, he said.
Not even your father.

When Mother called to say
he would not die,
I knew the opposite,
knew in my bones
the way his bones
would fill with disease
and in the end
how his eyes would glass over
with pain, like the eyes
of the mare we delivered
together one spring.

He brought me a playhouse—
a real log cabin,
one of the roadside cottages
that sat under shady trees
on the winding road to Chetek,
sold to make room
for a new motel.
A house of my own
for my whole childhood,
with a wide front porch
and green-checked curtains
at each sunny window.

He brought home delinquent
teenaged boys
I fell in love with.
There was dark-haired Vince,
bailed out of jail,
who worked in our yard
and wouldn't go to school.
Beautiful, dangerous Vince
with the silver belt,
the boy I wasn't allowed to follow.

Years after that I helped carry hay
to the horses in winter.
I worked in our small café,
where he greeted customers
with a whistle, remembering
for years who took cream
in his coffee—even strangers
who came for the summer fishing.
One cup, and he'd know forever.

He didn't come to my wedding,
such as it was—
quiet, one cold Wednesday.
Couldn't close the café,
he said.
But later gave me
the old blue Plymouth,
a box of groceries each time
we came home, and tuition,
and carried the baby happily
on his shoulder.

In Charleston,
the last year of his illness,
he could hardly sit in a car,
but seeing his first live oak
forgot the hours it took
to arrive.
While my brother sat
on a marvelous limb,
Dad put his hands on the trunk

and stood there in silence.
I thought of the trees
he'd planted,
and the ones he'd named.

When he asked to go home
for Christmas,
we bundled him into a borrowed van
that could hold a wheelchair,
and drove through town.
He wanted to see for the last time
the splendor of lights
transforming familiar streets,
making our town
a northern heaven.
We spoke of the years
he'd climbed through snow
to string the cedars
with blue.

But after one agonized night
and day, when we stood
in a circle around his bed
while the light came and went
with the pain,
we took him back
to the hospital,
against his will,
and there, three weeks later,
he left us, as people do.

FROM THE BEGINNING

Lifted into the arms of the world
we feel our safety slip
as one drunken foot beneath hurls

itself out, imagines we're dancing, trips
on the rolled-back, rose-swirled rug
and we almost fall. We feel the great heart skip

a beat, then speed, then clutch to hug
us closer. Too late. The baby we'll always be
knows that for years we'll tug

ourselves out of, into, beds, relieved
both when there's someone there, and alone,
sure that the end of every road is grief.

Even when we travel on old cobblestone
in the carriage of childish dreams
and sometimes see our ancestors' bones

in ours, sturdy, high and refined in the cheeks,
suggesting ancient wisdom, protection
against vague dangers we fear but cannot speak

of—deep down we believe it. The election
of souls is not so far in our past.
That Presbyterian predisposition

to think of death at every turn lasts
generations. We see ourselves ablaze,
not chosen. All those years wearing masks,

and when we take them off, nobody's saved,
as far as we can tell. Or saving is something
else, but not escape. Then—we're amazed

by love, and the luminous change it brings,
the sense that this must be salvation
or its closest twin. We're ready to fling

away what we've worked for hardest, the creation
of ourselves—those children we've taught to walk
alone on narrow bridges, solve problems of addition,

perspective, and plumbing, and how to talk
to strangers—in favor of it:
Love, which overcomes the shock

of its own power. Calmed, we decide this was written
somewhere inside. Even from the beginning.

FROM *The Swimmer* (1984)

YESTERDAY I SWAM IN THE RAIN

Water on water in perfect fusion,
light welded to shimmering light.
When the thunder started, and the lightning,
I tried to remember the horses my father lost
to a storm, struck in the nearest pasture.
Absorbed in the pleasure of water,
I had to work hard at fear, that dark savior,
to make myself head for shore.

SOME NOTES ON COURAGE

Think of a child who goes out
into the new neighborhood,
cap at an angle, and offers to lend
a baseball glove. He knows
how many traps there are—
his accent or his clothes, the club
already formed.
Think of a pregnant woman
whose first child died—
her history of blood.
Or your friend whose father
locked her in basements, closets,
cars. Now when she speaks
to strangers, she must have
all the windows open.
She forces herself indoors each day,
sheer will makes her climb the stairs.
And love. Imagine it. After all
those years in the circus, that last
bad fall when the net didn't hold.
Think of the ladder to the wire,
spotlights moving as you move,
then how you used to see yourself
balanced on the shiny air.
Think of doing it again.

I ARRIVE IN A SMALL BOAT, ALONE

In my bed your body is an island
inhabited by a cautious race of men
whose elaborate rituals were designed
for safety, like the shaking of hands
to show an absence of weapons,
or the sharing of food to prove its purity.
They are united, they rally
to a common cause, so that
when possible danger appears,
they line up, each with one knee
on the ground for balance,
shields side by side,
the reflected sun bright enough
to blind the approaching figure,
me, waving a hand.
Now and then one's caught by himself
off-duty, the tribe's chant
dim in the distance. Sometimes
he hears a song that seems
to come from his own blood's rhythm.
But he checks himself,
returns to the village quickly,
rarely tripping on roots,
for he's memorized the path,
cut away offending branches.
Safely back, he joins the others,
sleeps in his own hut, in tune
with the breath of his brothers.
He knows if he keeps still long enough
the music will stop.

TRYING TO COME TO TERMS

He says he's all darkness, wishes he could care.
I am not wanton, don't fling myself at men,
but fell into his arms as if despair

were the proper price. Now what I hastily spent
I want to earn back. Yet only small coins
rattle in my heart. I take up pen

and try to write it, to understand the point,
like peering through binoculars to the church
five miles away. The picture's out of joint

here in the mountain retreat where birch
and maple absorb the night sounds
of animals, of human grief. Later today I'll search

for the moth, note the beauty of the luna's down
against its ugly body, that iridescent green
pulsing its last on the log's crown

where I watched it yesterday. I'll look to trees
for answers, as if nature stored them up
to be discovered by any stray hiker, free.

This at a time when death's buzzing shop
is open all hours. Three friends give up the fight,
almost, with cancer. I have to work hard to stop

imagining them in a craftsman's hands, light
wood he carves into shapes, torsos of pain
whittled clean. Everywhere I look, tight-

lipped patients, doctors, families strain
for belief. But the miracles we half-expect of love
go whistling off on the nearest train,

denying failure. I put on the sterile gloves
and mask, tell myself this has nothing
to do with me. Then, shaken with fear, shove

the bouquets aside and admit it: breathing
is precious as any dream of the future.
Everything pales in the whispering,

the request for a simple back rub, a gesture
that's useful. I observe the odd fragrance, alcohol and sweat.
Something here is genuine. Not that mixture

of lust and need we grasp for and sometimes guess
is all. If there is anything like a way out,
it's discovered in rooms like these, pressed

as we are to be honest, at least to ourselves, about
love, though sickness keeps growing like doubt.

ANNE, DYING

Her body like a stubborn root
dug up and left in the air to dry
has survived and survived,
but now that will, like her caught breath,
is nearly gone.

Pain spills through her like blood
from the heart the cancer grows against,
surrounds, tough lilies of the valley
spreading until their sweetness
overpowers, crowding the bed
so nothing else can feel the sun.

Love comes trooping in with baskets
of white flowers, an awful innocence.
It fails. It masquerades as hope,
believes itself awhile, and in the end
does not save anyone.

THE MAN WHO BROUGHT THE GYPSY MOTH

I, Leopold Trouvelot, am guilty,
though I meant no crime, and could not imagine
the apple, basswood, poplar and willow
gone, had not foreseen the loss of hawthorn
and sassafras. Only the butternut
still stands in my old field, a sentinel,
and a single dogwood sighs near the house
we had to leave. My Boston neighbors believed
I was sent by the devil, but it isn't so.
No god, either. I alone am responsible.

I saw silk in my dreams, flowing blue silk
wrapped twice round Marie, trailing her down
the stairs like water. *To make silk*, I thought,
more perfect than petals.
I remember Marie in the yard after dinner,
her long hair wound at the base of her neck
like a rose. She loved the grape arbor
and that white clapboard house
so different from our cottage back home.
She was happy, and I, with my secret project,
rejoiced.

But in May, the white flowers on the shadbush
opened, the oak leaves unfurled,
and my small friends betrayed me.
As the air got warmer,
the town began to fill with black worms
blown tree to tree on the strands they'd spun,
and in weeks most all the leaves disappeared.
Not even Paris green deterred them.
One woman we knew scraped worms
from the sides of her house
and into a pan, poured kerosene over and set them
on fire. All day long she did this, weeping.

Even here in France I can't forget.
Those caterpillars with red and blue warts
became the most hated sight in New England—
next to me. In my nightmares, oak leaves turn
in an instant to excrement. Yet sometimes I still dream
of innocent moths that float through my nights
like cherry blossoms, of incredible silk
lovely as Marie.

DARWIN DISCOVERS THE GALAPAGOS

Finding this place was like falling
into the moon. As a child I'd lie
on the hill beside our house at dusk
watching it brighten, those craters
caves I ached to explore. I imagined
every shadow a mystery
longing for light.

Now here I am, off the coast of Ecuador,
where an archipelago of volcanos,
land pocked as that ancient face,
greets me like a dream
of all I ever knew.

It *must* have begun here,
where everything's moon and sea.
Look—that bird can't lift into air
but dives through water
for its prey, flies beneath the waves
as if the breakers were clouds.
Even the odd iguanas, those tiny dinosaurs,
swim.

How many million years?

Here, where the equator cuts through
like a current, these steamy islands
have kept the story whole. I almost believe
it *is* dream. In the mangrove forests,
on the beaches where each grain of sand
is white as a star, in the lagoons
with their pink flamingos rising
out of the mist, I sometimes
have to grab Fitz by the shoulder
and demand to know what he sees.

Confirmed, I go off alone
to sit on the rocks and watch the sea lions slide

from the shore, the giant tortoises drift by,
to think of the words I might use
to tell the world of the world.

CONQUERING THE NIGHT JASMINE

Beneath the dining room window
where everyone knows it should never
be grown, the night jasmine sends up
its devilish fragrance, sweet
as anything God imagined—
but with that telltale underscent
of abandon, of clove.

I must eat before eight each evening,
before it begins to exhale through the screen,
making the dinner inedible,
peas, lamb and rice all honeyed alike.

Plain as a weedy potato vine,
it looks innocent all day,
its silence a dare
to accuse or uproot it.

I wouldn't. I know temptation
when I see it, and how to pass such tests.

Cestrum nocturnum, Cestrum nocturnum,
I chant, and by nine it invades
the whole house, so all the air's sugary,
vulgar.

When I can bring
great panicles of the flowers in
as if they were fall hydrangeas, the tiny blooms
loose in Aunt Ellen's cranberry vase,
it will be victory.

I long for the hot summer night
I can keep my heart quiet
without the aid of marigolds.

MAN ARRESTED IN HACKING DEATH TELLS POLICE HE MISTOOK MOTHER-IN-LAW FOR RACCOON

Every morning she'd smear something brown
over her eyes, already bagged
and dark underneath, as if that would
get her sympathy. She never slept,
she said, but wandered like a phantom
through the yard. I knew it. Knew
how she knelt beneath our bedroom window too,
and listened to Janet and me.

One night when *again* Janet said No,
I called her a cow, said she might as well
be dead for all she was good to me.
The old lady had fur in her head
and in her ears,
at breakfast slipped and told us
she didn't think the cows would die.

Today when I caught her
in the garage at dawn, that dyed hair
growing out in stripes, eyes
like any animal surprised from sleep
or prowling where it shouldn't be,
I did think, for a minute,
she was the raider of the garden,
and the ax felt good, coming down
on a life like that.

AFTER WARNINGS FROM COUNTY PROSECUTOR MINISTER AGREES TO STOP USING ELECTRIC SHOCKS TO TEACH BIBLE STUDENTS

Tried half my life
to fuse flesh and spirit,
finally learned how.

Listen, it's the joy
of a dry dive
into spring-fed, icy water,
but better, the reverse—
hot as a fever dream.

One girl *begs* me for the juice,
says when He enters her like that,
it's the moon exploding.
I can see every nerve amazed
with exquisite pain,
and in a flash
she knows the universe
inside out.

I swear, it's *wrong, wrong*
to condemn pure Christian ecstasy
as if it were sin.

AFTER HE CALLED HER A WITCH

Special powers were attributed to the orange in Renaissance England, Italy, and Sicily.
It was believed witches could bring death to an enemy by pinning the victim's name
to an orange and leaving the orange in a chimney.

When he comes in, late again,
the whole house smells wonderful,
but he can't quite recognize the scent.
The fire is almost out, a few ashes
flicker in the absent light,
and suddenly he recalls
his mother holding orange peels
over a flame, the singed skin
curling back like petals,
releasing that fragrance.
She did it daily, all one winter,
just for the pleasure.

He doesn't see on the hearth
the remains of paper, traces
of his name printed in clear
black ink. He wonders how his wife
knew about sweetening their rooms
with oranges, wonders whether it means
the air is cleared,
she wants to make up.
He breathes the evening in,
imagining her in bed, waiting for him,
forgiveness on her lips
like the taste of oranges.

THE ARTIST

For Sheba Sharrow

She keeps her windows open,
refusing to fix the torn screen all summer.
Ignoring mosquitoes, she tolerates
brown-speckled spiders she finds
in her sheets, hoping for one small creature
banded in colors nobody's used.
She has learned to see in the faintest light
how the veins of a moth in Virginia
cross at angles different from all
she's observed, and in her absorption,
does not hear the man who slips out
of the woods, whose hands are like nets.
When he surprises her, cupping her breasts
from behind, she imagines, first,
that they're doves, and she sees them
on canvas, white feathers pulsing
against dark fingers.

CLEOPATRA

After the painting by Guido Reni

Asp bites nipple, no fooling around.
She's larger than love,
and when she turns that white face up,
one hand resting
in the basket of snakes and flowers,
the other guiding reptile to target
by its curly tail,
it's hard to think of Antony
caressing that ample skin.
She could be a saint.
Those pudgy fingers should fold
in prayer, not casually pluck a nut
as she holds the asp
like an awkward teacup.
Her passive mouth might never
have been kissed; those eyes, raised
heavenward, are the eyes
of a Georgia farmwife
claiming ecstasy, not knowing
quite what she's missed.

NOBLEMAN WITH HIS HAND
ON HIS CHEST

After the painting by El Greco

Sir, I too agree with Ignatius.
One should touch his heart at each sin,
and the remembrance of it.

But you are not penitent. Your eyes
have learned sadness,
how, by focusing on a spot in the glass,
you can say to yourself,
Here is a gentleman wan with grieving.
I am that man. Believe the fingers
resting on pain.

We know better, you and I.

You love how the white ruff circles,
how lace softens, flatters
that sternness, sets off
the appropriate black
beneath your somber face.

Your sins glitter like your sword,
ornate and handsome.
You take them out in the dark
to admire; in public, you
press them back into place.

THE GARDEN OF EARTHLY
DELIGHTS

After the painting by Hieronymus Bosch

So understandable that you
would seek birds,
with their fiery feet,
the yellow-striped plumes,
and beaks that curve and point
like graceful fingers.
Their plump throats pulse
the way your bodies should.
But your faces say something's wrong.
You rest on those feathery backs,
pondering. Even without each other
you should find pleasure
just sitting on such spiny softness.
Why the glum looks
when you've got what you wanted—
bodies naked as eggs—alabaster,
obsidian skin, yours for the touching,
the taking. You open
your ravenous mouths for sweet fruit,
and it's there. But your hearts
are cool as the water
where everyone rises to gorgeous sin.

KEEPING THE TRUTH ALIVE

After drawings by Henrich Kley

Before we settle in
let's find tiny elephants
to suckle me awhile,
and admit the lady was right
who saw the earth perched
on a turtle's back. To Wm. James,
who objected, politely asking
what the turtle stood on,
she sagely replied, "Ah,
it's no use, Mr. James.
It's turtles, all the way down."
The crafty penguin
serenading a woman on the ice,
an accordion of human bodies
moaning out of tune
as legs are split
and pumped together again,
even the rape by snail—
we've known them, known
what it's like to sit
on the sword's edge pleading,
or to hold a small squealing animal
by one leg in the air.
As the sated preacher sleeps
beneath the crucifix,
he dreams of real Christian poverty
and wakes aghast. We dream
what we can. With luck we might be
the naked couple straddling
the Orient Express
still bound for Paris.

THE CROSSING

To find, across the bridge of night,
one constant voice urging you over,
telling you where the loose stones are,
where the missing beam, you must
be willing to risk that journey
with your eyes blindfolded, your hands
in gloves. You must believe that close
on the other side is a room
prepared only for you. There a small
blue lamp will be shining, and books
piled on the table, ones you've
longed for, but nearly forgot.
All the while you're crossing, feet
hesitant and chilled, you must imagine
a high four-poster bed, layers
of quilts, that voice become a murmur,
the river at your back.

ENCOUNTER AT THE HARBOR

Everyone who made you what you are
appears in windows along the waterfront,
each with his own story, her own wish
for forgiveness. Your father
tells the assembly how you played
a music box over and over
until he thought he'd go mad
with the sweet tinny sound.
The nun who insisted you write
blasphemy a hundred times on the blackboard
drops her spectacles to the sidewalk,
urging the crowd to applaud as they shatter.
Your brother confirms his fascination
with your skin, how he teased you to silence,
making you let him touch you all over.
Someone recites a list of confessions,
why he invented a trip to Boston,
then disappeared like a pond in summer.
You stand before them dressed in white,
your face impassive as dawn.
Only when they weep in chorus
do you turn to the bay, point out
how the sun rises behind the island.

THE SWIMMER

Imagine yourself a strong swimmer.
Instead of that awkward crawl to the raft,
you can go all the way out, then down to the dam
half a mile away. There's nothing in sight
to disturb you. No shiny rowboats, no walkers
along the shore like sentinels.
No sign of rain or shudder of thunder.
Only the gentlest ripples alter the surface,
the ghost of a breeze. You can keep on swimming
until the sun goes out like a candle.
Under that starry sky, you'll float
in the shadows of shadows.
There might be no end to it, just water
darkening into night, then slowly restoring itself
to blue. The silence will be a new entrance
to dreams, sleep a new way to breathe.

FROM *Northern Lights* (1981)

LESSON

My father said quicksand
might be hidden in the tall swamp-grass,
would suck me down, down
to the center of earth.
Even in fall, the dry season,
when the horses snapped reeds
with each step,
a fearful swarm of insects
could mean that pit,
wet as fresh manure, was only disguised,
leaves covering it over like a blind.
Mother, no Ceres, did not believe
I would disappear. Watch
for blackbirds, she said,
handing me the old wicker basket.
Wherever they land is safe.
Bring me the small blue flowers
that grow close to the ground
and the tallest cattails
you can find.
I followed those redwings in,
feeling like Gretel, whistling for courage.
When I came out,
a mass of cattails over my shoulder
like a bag of gold,
basket filled with blossoms,
she was waiting at the edge,
waving and smiling.

THE PUNISHMENT

Remember the tree, Charlie?
Where I tied you with ropes
wound from your shoulders
all the way down
to your skinny ankles
like a loose-wrapped mummy?
And then took the branches
lying on the ground
and stuffed them
between you and the ropes
like jail bars,
not to help hold you in,
but to scratch you?
Weeks earlier, Grandma told me
you went to the hospital
with a broken arm,
claiming I did it
because you tried to kiss me.
I would have,
but that's not how it happened
and I've always been a fiend
for truth.
You cried, but not enough,
so I took another leafy branch
and whipped you. And when
I finally turned you loose,
the welts blossoming
on your arms and legs
like roses,
your tears did not move me
at all. I could still see you
at the emergency room,
grinning, arm in a sling,
selling stories to the nurses
that sent them out laughing,
repeating my innocent name.

LITTLE WOMEN

There in the playhouse,
making pies of flour and water
and apples from the neighbor's yard,
we learned to handle anything—
husbands who stopped in
just long enough
to sample the cookies,
gardens that washed away
in the first spring storm,
and babies crying,
their mechanical wails
stuck in their throats
like dimes. Sometimes
we thought we'd try something
else—I'd be
a missionary in Africa,
and a ballet dancer,
and go to Mars.
I remember standing on the sidewalk,
hands raised to the sky,
proclaiming I would not
be married, have children,
live in a neighborhood
like this. But always
we returned
to the little house
behind my real one,
put on the long dresses
with folds that wrapped us
like gifts,
the shiny high heels,
and the feathered hats.
Then we practiced
a dignified walk
around and around the block.

BURIALS

The difficulties of hiding anything.
How for a child, it all seems easy.
I had a room behind my room,
a space back of the built-in drawers
next to the closet. I could
take a drawer out, crawl through,
and ease it back like a piece
in a puzzle. With a flashlight,
books, the world was safe as Freiberg
before the war.
I kept my valuables there:
cigar boxes full of bottle caps
(worth money then—some kind of contest),
a pile of comics, the antique china doll
whose legs and arms I snapped one day
for spite.

Today I look through a notebook.
It has my name, but I know
none of this. Some of the words
I can't define, and books I discuss
I don't remember reading.
The writing is small and neat
like my aunt's. It almost draws pictures.

Sometimes even my face is a surprise.
I walk out happy, but someone comes up
on the street and asks what's wrong.
I think of last night's dream:
my father alive again at the table,
a baby crying, pages falling from the sky
like rain, and then like leaves
needing to be raked, put in order.
I can see which way the signs point,
but who would want to go there?

MOTHERHOOD

Think of gentleness, as when
a head lifts and nods to a child,
easy permission. I remember
going back and forth to the kitchen
in winter, where the oven held us
like small lovely moths to the light.
Mother would hand us warm bread
with jelly, and we'd flit away
until we were cold again.

Now all my gestures are lost.
Too late for a bowl of cookies,
a hug, to make any difference.
He's younger in my dreams,
sometimes a brother. I walk out
to the barn to find the mare
I love, to give it to him.
But he can't understand,
and thinks she's dangerous.

I would begin again, have children
late, when I've learned
not to rely on words but on
bread rising each Saturday
in a life that would stay
as firm as a boy's deliberate stride
onto the soccer field.
I'd know what can be forgiven,
what grace warms the air like steam.

ALL MY ORIFICES ARE TOO SMALL

You laugh when I tell you, but it is truth.
Countless physicians have affirmed it, according
to their various specialties. The oral surgeon,
removing my five wisdom teeth (Yes, there really
were five. Some people, he said, grow eight,
two where normal people have one, upper and lower,
right and left. My extra one was upper left)
remarked that my mouth was extraordinarily small.
Friends snickered, but I had known for some time.
A grinning orthodontist, when I was twelve, insisted
that my oral cavity would not accommodate everything
necessary, and he removed four large and perfectly
healthy canines. And then there have been the matters
of ears and nose, so easily irritated by the tiniest
foreign matter. Oh, the hours I've spent draining
those narrow tubes. Though delicacy prevents my going
into detail, hemorrhoids are another
manifestation. Gynecologists, too, acknowledged
that a head would be hard pressed to make it through *that*
passage. And they were right. The alternative
was not entirely pleasant, and I no longer wear
bikinis, but there are obvious compensations.
Some of us will do anything to assert our
individuality. I do not maintain, of course,
that these problems are totally distinctive, but
you will have to admit, my claim is somewhat unique.

AGAIN, FATHER, THAT DREAM

Leading the saddled pony back
to find its frightened rider, I see
a café, drift in for a cup of coffee.
Those plain white porcelain mugs
undo me again, I cannot drink
or have a conversation
without the sound of your voice
calling *Mabel, Mabel* into the kitchen,
Mother coming out, shy and hesitant,
hiding her spattered apron
with her hands. I hear you
whistling, that warble
rising on the air of this strange
place like finches suddenly let in.
The others do not notice.
The radio comes on, a ballgame,
and I remember the pony, tied
outside, far from the lost child.

TALE FOR A DAUGHTER

We knew what cold was. Each morning Dad rode a horse
to the auction barn at the edge of town, then walked the
rest of the way to work. After school I'd meet him at the
shop, and when he finished sweeping up, we half-ran (my
long strides matching his) the mile or so to where he'd
left the gray, whose mane and forelock by then were ice,
like foil you hang on a Christmas tree. When he pulled
me up behind him, the horse dancing a circle on the
slippery road, I became a Norwegian pioneer, romantic
and tough like my grandmother. All the way home my
mittened hands, clasped round my father's middle, felt
ready to crack, to break off at the wrists like an electric
cord snaps at 40 below when you touch it. Behind his
wide back that blocked the wind, my face and body were
warmer, and the horse's heat as we galloped spread into
my thighs, teaching me early what women must learn,
one way or another, about survival.

THE CHILD'S DREAM

If I could start my life again,
I'd keep the notebook
I promised myself at nine—
a record of all the injustice
done by adults: that accusing tone
when they speak, the embarrassments
before relatives, like the time
I had to put on my swimsuit in the car
while Mother chatted with an uncle
who peered in, teasing.
And *wouldn't* they be sorry
later, when they read it,
after I'd been run over by a truck,
their faces darkening
like winter afternoons.
And I, of course (if I survived),
would have a reminder,
in my own hand,
so I'd be the perfect parent,
my children radiant as the northern lights.
It's like poems you hope
will be read by someone who knows
they're for him, and cry
at what he did or didn't do,
wishing to touch your face once more,
to cradle your body.
You can almost hear what he'd tell you
with his voice that sounds
like the sea rolling in
over and over, like a song.

GOOD CHILD

I am concerned that when you leave here today your
daughter will go crazy again. And I think the reason
she will do it is to save your marriage.
—from an article by Janet Malcolm in
The New Yorker

Now the slightest touch of the breeze
to a branch, the rattle of leaves
on my window, and the glass gets
brittle, threatens to disintegrate.
The piano plays itself in my dreams,
always a frenzied tune,
and voices of friends have turned
animal, my fear making them
vicious, bullying. When I speak
Mother does not hear the words
at all, but Father locks himself
away. I find old letters I wrote
from camp, letters they saved
in the desk drawer. I rewrite them
telling the truth: I am not
having fun. Each day the lake
gets deeper, and my breath
no stronger. I dive for rocks
covered in tinfoil, but when
I come up, my hands are empty,
the others win the prizes.
Today I walked the lane
to our old house.
The trees were down in the coming wind
and I could hear hail before it fell.

ON LEARNING THAT CERTAIN PEAT BOGS CONTAIN PERFECTLY PRESERVED BODIES

Under this town's ashes
lies a man, still sweating
the long summer days,
his body
perfect as morning,
even to the bacon and eggs
in his belly.
His skin is damp
in the humid earth,
closed eyes heavier
under rain.
The heart quit pumping early,
but when a rock eases down
and cuts an arm
or grazes his back,
blood still seeps
from the veins,
the clots blooming
like poppies around him.
In the brain
memories lie opened,
one into the other:
the crunch of the ax
as he swings down hard,
his wife calling his name
in the distance.
He does not hear them,
but they are there,
claiming their portions.
By now the wife may be
dead too, the ax passed down
to his son, or rusted

under the woodpile.
The woman cannot recall
her own clear voice
or the features of the man
who should be bones.

THE KISS

A mother of two is so allergic to the bite of an inch-
long insect called the kissing bug, she faces death
unless someone starts producing more antigen (a
liquid medicine made from the bugs) to counter-
act the bites. For the present, research money has
run out.
                              —*Los Angeles Times*

She does not hear him
ascend the leg of her bed
as if it were a mountain
where at the top, only at the top,
the sweetest berries grow.

He is relentless as a child
who could wait all morning in silence
piling and unpiling blocks in the corner
for a reward like this.

He stops a moment, puffs his small
pink belly as the bed trembles
with her breathing.

Finally he slips
into the fragrant sheets
and waits for a smooth breast
to flatten on its side
as she shifts position.
Some of his brothers
were frozen alive,
their bodies dissolved even now,
perhaps, in her blood.

But it is not revenge he is after.

He wants only to taste her,
to feel his power
swell with her fear, to sing
the song of her life.

JEANNE D'ARC

To be chosen—

my small body rejoices
at the words,
encases itself in silver
more lovely than silk.

Not to stay in the village
and marry the miller,
his babies heavy in my arms
as loaves of bread—

not to be God's bride
dressed in the long black robe
I've secretly named a shroud,
needing always to chasten myself
for my shimmering dreams—

but Christ's innocent mistress,
Lily of War!

Still, I can scarcely believe
how each time I speak
the sky brightens.

When the voice first came
from behind the dark trees
I sat for a long time, trembling.
Now my skin
burns, imagining how it will be,
the horse between my thighs,
a thousand men behind me,
singing.

THE WIDOW

A stranger arrives at her door
in a T-shirt, his truck
parked outside like a sign:
This is an honest repairman.
He wants directions, but she
does not know the street.
When he asks to use the phone,
she lets him into the kitchen
where the water has just begun
to boil, steaming the windows
like breath.

She remembers the novel
where a man holds a knife
to a child's small throat,
drawing a thin line of blood,
then takes the young mother
off in his truck to rape her.
She thinks where her knives are,
imagines throwing the water
straight from the stove
in his face.

He murmurs something
into the phone.
She has gone to another room
and can't make out the words,
the tone is too soft,
but she hears the water
boil over, spatter the gleaming
stainless steel of her range
like the hiss of firecrackers
before they explode.
He pulls the pan off the burner,
calls to her,
Lady? Lady?

She hides in the bathroom,
listens, even after she hears
the door open again, and close
like the click of a trigger.
When at last the truck
pulls away, she comes out,
spends the whole afternoon
drifting back and forth
to the window.

Making supper,
she burns her hand,
cries softly
long after the pain is gone.

The next morning, she's amazed
to see she'd forgotten
to lock the back door,
to turn off the lights
that burned all night
in the kitchen.

MARGARET

Mrs. A. J. Cowles, aged 87 years, died at Beloit. She had been married to Deacon Cowles, who survives her, for nearly 68 years. On the occasion of her last birthday her eccentric husband presented her with a coffin which he had made with his own hands and in which she was buried.

—March 16, 1893, *Badger State Banner*

All these months I've polished it
with good wax, made him see
I loved the smooth grain,
the rich finish.
I'd been too well to think of it
as bed, but at the first ache
he removed the plants I'd put on top.
Now, lying here, seeing it open,
I try to admire the well-sealed joints,
the whorled pattern on the inside lid,
but I am irritable, ungrateful.
I pray, but God must know.
Last night I dreamed
I locked myself in the pantry.
The neighbors tried to let me out
but the spring floods came
and they all left in boats.
This morning
the pain is no worse than ever
but I keep drowsing off
and I wake up crying.

MARY

Mary Ricks, the Wisconsin window-smasher, has put in an appearance at Eau Claire. She was taken into custody by a policeman as she was about to wreck a fine plate glass window.
—February 22, 1894, *Badger State Banner*

It was *so clean*. Mother used to say
if you polish one like that
a man might walk through it,
thinking it a clear passage
to the garden, but be surprised
by the crack and the instantaneous
shock of something slicing his shoulder,
his belly, so that the blood
would run from here to Lake Michigan.
Sometimes I stand outside a greenhouse.
Cardinals batter themselves
on the roof, the sides.
Sometimes I find a sparrow
with a broken neck, but never
any blood. Mother was wrong.
Nobody bleeds but me.
I try to wait till after dark
on the main streets,
but when I can't, someone
always comes too soon. Still,
I have plenty of scars,
and in jail they bring bandages,
are usually gentle with wounds.

VICTORIA

Victoria Hanna, a middle-aged woman of Kaukauna,
Outgamie County, was bound over to Commissioner
Bloodgood the other day in the sum of $500 on the
charge of sending obscene matter through the mails.
The woman had a spite against a neighbor and mailed
her a letter of the filthiest description.
    —May 14, 1885, *Badger State Banner*

Dear Mrs. Anderson,

Your Lars came to my house again
last night, wearing his dung overalls,
and when I heard him brush the hedge
under my window, I sent out the dog.
You think I make this up because
you have hair like my sister Bertie,
but I tell you, he's here
more than twice a week.
Sometimes I pretend I don't know.
I slip my chemise off
slowly, as if I'm so weary
I can hardly stretch my arms.
(And in the moonlight I know
how white my skin is,
how lean, even now, my body.)
Sometimes I complain of the heat
and pull everything off,
stretch on the bed,
my legs and arms flung wide,
wishing aloud for a fan
or someone to fan me.
Then I get up
and dust myself, breast to toe,
with strawberry talcum.

I always hear the swish of leaves outside.

But last night I got tired
of the game, tired of your tolerant smile
every time you see me.
This time, just check the right leg

of his barn pants.
I can see you sitting there
in your parlor,
your thin lips drawn
to a line as straight as the seam
you'll sew. You with your
snaky black hair.
You with your pity.

MINNIE

Miss Minnie Rose of Beaver Dam shot herself in the
Plankinton House in Milwaukee. She left a letter in
which she asks that her body be destroyed by elec-
tricity. . . . In the letter she says that untrue stories
circulated about her drove her to suicide.
                    —December 29, 1898, *Badger State Banner*

I wanted the same room
on the fourth floor,
the one in the corner
with the oak by the window,
but it was taken.
I'd planned to sit
in the green velvet chair
where he held me on his lap,
said I shocked him with my tongue.
All that talk of hot wires
and currents and volts
he said I made him feel,
I began to think I was dangerous.
Shouldn't touch you
when I'm wet, I said,
and he laughed and laughed,
the dark hairs on his arms
almost crackling.

He should have been a stranger
riding from town to town
through the worst summer storms,
not plain old Ruth Peterson's husband,
who died pinned under a wagon.

BREASTS

The first time they mattered
I was eleven, drying the dishes,
when my little brother
folded me into a chair
with a jab—
a pain so deep I knew
he'd stopped my heart.
That was before I'd even noticed
them growing. Later, wishing
them large as moons, I treasured
their tenderness,
pressed the swollen sides
with my fingers, the way
I love now, you firming the flesh
as a sculptor fondles soft clay.
When did I learn the pleasure
of one entirely embraced by a hand,
nippling the palm,
the other begging?
As you enter the room, they grow warm,
lift toward the sun like small flowers.
I follow, their sure direction
taking us somewhere we've been.
Again, something stops my breath
like a fist, but the heart
knows its part, does not frighten me now
with its long, deliberate pause.

ALL I EVER WANTED WAS A GOD

I keep trying to be Leda,
but no one presses his feathers
hard on my thighs; no one
catches my hair in his beak,
pulling me hot through the sky.
Nobody even gets jealous
of the birds I keep caged.
I'd like to pretend indifference,
but the ponds of my dreams
keep filling with swans,
and my rationalizations—
          the men I've loved rarely
          had hollow bones, and
          Olympians frequently make
          bad husbands, and who, after all,
          would really want Helen
          for a daughter—
just sound like sour grapes.

A BARGAIN AT ANY PRICE

Daily I go to the carpet warehouse.
The men think I can't make up my mind.
But the truth is, I have fallen in love
with the young ex–football player
who lights the dingy room with his hair.
Even machines can't help him add,
so we spend hours figuring and refiguring
costs—pad and labor, stairs and tax,
his patient golden head bent over the numbers,
the muscles in his arms reflecting shadows
like water under summer clouds.
Each time he starts the motor on the forklift,
slowly pushing that long steel rod
into the center of a roll, then
lifting it out for me to see, oh—
it's as if an inner sky were opening,
and all his hazy calculations
fall like stars into my heart.

TRYING TO CHANGE
THE SUBJECT

I have sworn to quit
inviting antelope
and elk
into my small backyard,
but the bear refuses
to stop wandering in.
His fur
always gets caught
in the gate
and his steps
on the porch
rattle the glasses
in my cupboard.
Each time he comes
the dog is nervous
for a week.
When he ate my blackberries
I said it didn't matter
but in fact
I had nothing to eat
all day. Yet
when I tell him
I've decided against him,
he laughs,
batting my wind chimes
with his paw.

THE WISDOM

Find the island. You will know it
for the shore is too rocky for landings
and a yellow flag waves from the peak
of its one small mountain. Go there
by balloon. The balloon must be striped
and of many colors. I have seen
the perfect one floating near
my house. We can find its owner
together, and he will give it
gladly. When you land
use the silk for adornment.
You will not need a house or a hut
or clothing, for the weather is perfect
always. And when one evening you hear
the voices of children, I will come.
We will begin to discover
the wisdom, to create the seasons.